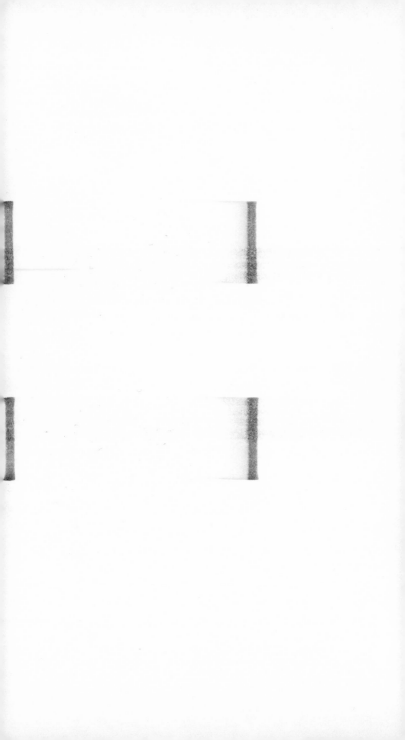

ALSO BY HARRIETTE COLE

Choosing Truth: Living an Authentic Life

Coming Together: Celebrations for African American Families

How to Be: Contemporary Etiquette for African Americans

Jumping the Broom: The African-American Wedding Planner

Jumping the Broom Wedding Workbook:
A Step-by-Step Write-in Guide for Planning
the Perfect African-American Wedding

Vows

The African-American
Couples' Guide to Designing
a Sacred Ceremony

HARRIETTE COLE

Simon & Schuster Paperbacks

New York   London   Toronto   Sydney

SIMON & SCHUSTER PAPERBACKS
Rockefeller Center
1230 Avenue of the Americas
New York, NY 10020

First Simon & Schuster paperback edition 2005

SIMON & SCHUSTER PAPERBACKS and colophon are registered trademarks
of Simon & Schuster, Inc.

For information regarding special discounts for bulk purchases,
please contact Simon & Schuster Special Sales:
1-800-456-6798 or business@simonandschuster.com

Designed by Liney Li

Manufactured in the United States of America

10   9   8   7   6   5   4   3   2   1

The Library of Congress has cataloged the hardcover edition as follows:
Cole, Harriette.
   Vows : the African-American couples' guide to designing a sacred
ceremony / Harriette Cole.
       p.   cm.
   Includes bibliographical references and index.
   1. Marriage service.   2. Marriage customs and rites.
3. African Americans.   I. Title.

HQ745.C653   2004
392.5'089'96073—dc22   2003066783

ISBN 0-684-87313-3
       0-684-87314-1 (Pbk)

I dedicate this book of Vows

to my husband and life partner, George Chinsee.

With him at my side and in my heart,

I am discovering how to become a greater Me,

a better partner, and a more capable servant

in this exquisite world in which we live.

I know that I am blessed

to have found this great man

with whom to share my life.

I love you, Chinsee!

CONTENTS

A Note of Thanks   xi

The Pledge of Partnership   1

Reflecting on Your Commitment   5

Embracing Your Heritage   17

The Value of Marriage   37

Elements of Your Sacred Ceremony   55

Ceremonial Rituals from Around the World   89

Selecting Your Officiant   109

Writing Your Own Wedding Vows   125

Your Wedding Party: Inspiring Others to Serve   145

Welcoming Children into the Ceremony   161

Renewing Your Vows   167

Starting Over   179

Joining Ceremonies   185

End Note   193

The Creative Team   195

Bibliography   197

Index   199

A NOTE OF THANKS

Creating *Vows* came as the result of observation—of seeing many couples live in uplifting marriages and others who suffered through silent pain. *Vows* emerged thanks to couples' telling the truth about how they came together as one. As people have shared their honest stories of the importance of paying attention to the details of getting married, I have noticed a pattern emerging. Paying attention is important.

Listening and observing others is vital as well. That's why I am so grateful for the many voices and lives that I have observed and whose stories find their way into this book.

I first want to thank my parents, Doris Freeland Cole and the late Harry Augustus Cole, who were married for forty-one years before my father passed, for showing me that marriage isn't perfect but that it's a choice that you make in your heart that can last if you choose to nurture it.

I thank my husband, George Chinsee, who believed in me from the moment we met and who has demonstrated patience, commitment, and faith in us ever since.

I remember Aunt Etta and Uncle Ted, who were married for sixty-two years before Uncle Ted passed away. Without children, this couple demonstrated that it was possible to find a rhythm between them that could and would sustain them in this life and beyond.

I think of Aunt Audrey and Uncle Henry, who took care of

my sisters and me when we were growing up. They showed us that partnership can have many personalities as long as it is infused with an unwavering loyalty and trust.

I celebrate Peggy and Lloyd Toone, dear friends of George and mine. These two show how in the midst of what may seem like a jet-setting life, devotion and commitment shine through above all, making it possible to experience love on its most fundamental and all-encompassing level.

I appreciate the generosity of my dear friend Jocelyn Cooper-Halliburton and her husband, Christopher Halliburton, who welcomed us into their home to photograph so many of the images that appear in this book.

I acknowledge the many couples who shared details of their weddings and their marriages with me. Your insights have mattered tremendously, adding rich fuel to the fire of commitment that burns brightly at the time of a wedding.

I also thank my editor, Sydny Miner, whose patience and skill have helped me to bring this book to life; and my agent, Madeleine Morel, for always believing in the projects I choose to pursue.

I thank everyone whose efforts and good wishes have touched this book. Your openness and blessings have made it a delight to complete.

With love,
harriette

Vows

The Pledge of Partnership

HE MOMENT you officially declare your love and commitment for one another will echo in your memory for years to come. The day, the time, the ambiance, the guests, the flowers—everything contributes to making your wedding a beautiful experience. You likely will spend countless hours in preparation for your big day. When your wedding day or collection of days comes, you will discover that the moment when you actually become married is precious and fleeting. Indeed, the wedding ceremony itself is but a part of the celebration.

This book is dedicated to that sacred space of time when you and your beloved become one as partners on life's grand journey. What's amazing is that no matter what your religion or family background, the wedding ceremony itself is generally quite simple. The components are basic: In the company of witnesses—usually members of your spiritual, familial, and social communities—you stand before one another and pledge to spend your lives together. In the tradition of our African ancestors, what makes a union sacred is standing before God, your loved ones, and the ancestors, creating a covenant of strength and integrity that will support you in the days to come. You commonly offer each other a symbol of your love—a ring or other piece of jewelry. You state your commitment using words that have resonated throughout the ages as a pledge to marriage, or through words of your own choosing. And then you celebrate with your loved ones, sealing the union with the breaking of bread.

So why a book about the sacred ceremony? Having been married for more than ten years now, as well as having produced numerous weddings for couples and advised on even more, I see how powerful and ephemeral the moment of commitment can be. I recognize how easy (and common) it is for couples to leave the details of the ceremony to the celebrant while they focus on the rest—everything from the clothing to the feast and entertainment. I see how the very reason for having a sumptuous celebration often gets swallowed up in the magnitude of the planning. And I understand how important it is for couples to slow down long enough to pay attention to what really matters at the heart of this day: their commitment to one another.

I encourage each of you to take the time to contemplate what

. . . .

your marriage will mean as your life together unfolds. Before you get caught up in the busyness of planning an event large or small, focus on the two of you. Reflect on what this union means and how you intend to nurture it, to put each other first, so that it will blossom into a life worth living.

When you take the time to consider how to capture the essence of your union in a sacred event, your unique wedding will come to life. Each aspect of your wedding ceremony is special. The readings that you include will illuminate the road you already have begun to travel. The people you invite to stand up with you at this pivotal time may make all the difference at a key moment further along your life's journey. The rituals you incorporate into the ceremony itself will help define your bond as they guide you into the future. The invocation of the ancestors will support you now and in times to come. The words that you speak to each other as vows of your love will stay in your hearts forever. Give yourself and your beloved the gift of making every facet of your joining sacred. You are worth it.

Whether your wedding ceremony lasts for less than an hour or stretches over the course of several days, *Vows* is designed to help bring your vision to life.

I wish you a lifetime of happiness, patience, respect, and trust. May it begin now as you plan to honor your commitment by designing your own sacred ceremony.

With great love,
harriette

. . . .

Reflecting on Your Commitment

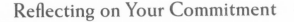

I'VE SPENT a lot of time talking with couples who are married as well as with those who are planning to marry. My great curiosity has been about what makes a marriage last. We know that statistics tell us to take heed: About 50 percent of all marriages in America end in divorce. How shall we consider this statistic? Some long-married couples and clerics take the high road. Looking at the glass as half full, they marvel that many couples remain steadfast in their pledges to one another in a culture that lives on fast-food thinking and lures people toward quick fixes and the ever present need for change.

My research shows that the couples who make it are the ones who decide from the start (and continue to make that choice) that they are in a partnership. There's a reason why many wedding vows speak of "through sickness and in health" and "for richer or poorer." Life doesn't follow the plan that we've had in our heads from childhood—or even from last year. Yes, it's important to create a road map for our lives. And it's also vital to remember that the road may curve differently than we intended. When we travel that road with a partner, we must bear in mind that their companionship can be a great gift and a challenge along the way. I spoke to Wilbur Levin, county clerk, Kings County, Brooklyn, New York; he occasionally officiates at civil ceremonies. Married for sixty years, Levin speaks of marriage both eloquently and practically. He says, "You have to work hard to make a marriage a success. The dividends from a happy marriage far exceed the dividends from anything else you do in life. It behooves you to work hard at it." He continues, "People should know that not everything is going to go well. Life can deal some terrible blows to people. There are all kinds of trials and tribulations that come your way when you're married, and no one has a pat hand. You have to know that if you're going to get married, it's going to happen and you have to be prepared to cope with it together as a team. That's what you are pledging to do, and if you don't mean to do it, then you really shouldn't get married."

Getting married is a sacred and sober experience. The goal

of marriage is to join two well-suited people together for life in a bond of love, trust, fidelity, and happiness. Perhaps the most important action you can take before getting married is to reflect on your commitment and honestly consider if you are ready for married life. Reverend Calvin O. Butts, of the world renowned Abyssinian Baptist Church in Harlem, says that many couples today don't have a clue as to what marriage means. Often they are so excited about the physical aspect of their relationship and about how much fun they are having that they don't stop to consider the emotional and moral maturity involved. Having pastored hundreds of married couples as well as being married more than thirty years himself, Butts knows of what he speaks.

Before sealing your union, look beyond the romantic and physical feelings to what it means to live together every day.

Do this through daily contemplation and journaling. Both of you can begin journals to be devoted solely to the exploration of your life together. From the moment that the two of you begin to discuss marriage, even if your discussion is as straightforward as, "Will you marry me?" followed by, "Yes," begin this exploration. Why? You want to make it your business to understand what yes means to each of you. So often people make the assumption that the way they believe is the way their partner believes. That simply isn't so. Each of us grows up with a particular value system, spiritual foundation, and way of looking at the world. Outline what you believe your way of under-

standing the world is, including your expectations of marriage—your role, your partner's role, your duties and responsibilities, as well as your partner's. Be clear and precise as you
make your list.

Premarital counseling is a good way to support your choice
to marry. If you are planning to marry within the context of a
spiritual tradition, your officiant likely will require that you engage in counseling with him or her. If you are having a secular
wedding, reach out to a therapist, minister, or other trained person to discuss your life's goals and intentions. This is a vital part
of establishing the foundation of your relationship. Many couples have found that they've been able to work through serious
issues early on that have saved them agony later down the line.
Others have decided not to marry based on the challenges they
were unable to overcome during their counseling sessions.

To give you a sense of what to expect during spiritual premarital counseling, Reverend James Forbes of the Riverside
Church in Harlem shares the substance of the process through
which he takes couples. Reverend Forbes believes it's essential
that you look honestly at your individual selves to discover who
you are, what your values are, and how well you mesh *before* you
decide to marry. He says, "Because couples are now basically
navel-gazing at each other, they tend sometimes to forget
about the larger context. You don't just marry couples, you
marry the couple's families and friends." Topics and issues

· · · · · · · · · · ·

Forbes explores and discusses with the couple include the definition of love, personal and family backgrounds, communication, personality traits, family and friends, finances, and faith— for example:

- Describe your background up to this point. Listen to each other as you share your stories.
- Share your family history. How many siblings do you have, and what are your relationships with them? Describe your relationship with your parents. What was it like growing up in your home? What values did you learn there?
- How comfortable are you listening to your partner share his or her life history? Do you provide encouragement, or are you judgmental?
- Do you genuinely love each other? How do you understand that love? How do you express it?
- How do you define romantic love in general and specifically in your relationship? What do you like, and what troubles you in this area? What do you expect from each other as lovers?
- Does your concept of love have any space for the acknowledgment of the dissatisfactions that come in life? Can you give examples of how you love during conflict?
- In what way is your love rooted and grounded in your experience of God's love for you?

. . . .

- Do you love yourself? How would you describe self-love in your own life? Do you think it's important to love yourself as you prepare for marriage?

- How do you communicate with one another? Is one of you talkative and the other quiet? How satisfied are you with the way your partner handles conflict?

- How do you deal with intense pleasure or satisfaction? Do you share the high points? If so, how well do you do that? Do you celebrate with each other?

- What are the defining characteristics of your style of communication? Is there anything you would like to change or that your partner would like for you to change?

- Could you stand your partner if he or she never changed a thing? How much do you grant your partner freedom for his own friends or her own friends? What standards of intimacy do you have? What would be a violation of the freedom in relationships? Female friends? What about male friends? After work?

- Do you know the point at which you have violated the expectations of the other?

- Must your friendships overlap? Can they be separate? How about family?

- Do you enjoy being with family? Can you handle the negativity that may come from different family members about your partner or your relationship—among them, the notion of this man stealing their lonely little pearl!

. . . .

♦ Now it's time to talk about finances and your relationship with money. What are your expectations about how your expenses will be handled? Who is responsible for what? Will you share your resources?

♦ Do you have shared or differing perspectives on material things? What about your differences in taste? What's your concept of waste? What kind of frugality are you hoping for from your mate?

♦ Do you want to go first class just because you can, or do you want to go coach even if you could afford first class?

♦ How many homes do you need? How many cars? Will you have the same bank account? Are you going to share? Is it all right for the woman to have some mad money? Is it all right for the man to have some mad money? Will you vacation together? How do you feel about separate vacations?

♦ Regarding your faith, what is your religious background? What do you intend for it to be if you hope to be together? If you are of the same denomination, the same faith tradition, how will you protect the freedom of the other? How will you share in the richness of the other person's practices if you do not share a faith tradition? What about your children? What are the means by which you as a family will renew your spiritual resources?

♦ Will you have prayer at home? Will you have a regular Bible reading? Will you go to church together? How do you plan to nourish the invisible dimension that probably has more

• • • • • • • • • • •

to do than the visible one with how your love is going to be sustained? How do you work through that kind of thing?

◆ Do you have any specific requests about the service for your wedding?

◆ What vows would you like to say? If you intend to write your own vows, what message do you want to convey?

You can reflect on and answer these questions in advance of a counseling session. Discuss them with your prospective mate. You can write in your journal to explore your thoughts and feelings. Whether you participate in this exercise singly or together, give yourselves the gift of talking them out with an adviser as well. Someone trained in counseling couples as they contemplate marriage can be useful in helping you to unmask any lingering issues you may have and provide a clear-eyed view of what your life together may be like. By doing so you will be clarifying your conviction to marry and fortifying your commitment.

As your vision of your life together crystallizes, you also will begin to recognize what images and words best describe your relationship. Write them down as precisely as you can. Make the effort to paint a picture with your words that illustrates what's unique about your relationship. These words will come in handy if you choose to write your own vows. They may also find their way into your wedding program, favors, and other items that you include in your wedding.

. . . .

❖ Declaring Your Intentions

Once you are clear about your intentions, share them with your loved ones. Although it may seem difficult to wait after he pops the question (or however you two come to the understanding that you want to marry!), do yourselves a favor and hold onto a private block of time when you sit with it and observe each other. When you are ready, with clear focus and resolve, spread the good news. Be mindful that you intend to create a sacred ceremony to honor your union, which means that you won't want to invite everybody you know. For this reason, it's wise to be mindful also of whom you tell the news to. If you share it personally with everyone who somehow touches your world, but you know you don't plan to invite all of those people, later down the line you face a dilemma. Expectations and hurt feelings can be avoided if you are thoughtful about your announcement.

When you do tell others, share your joy and vision for your wedding with reserve. Remember, this is *your* big day. Until you have all of the plans in place, keep your deepest feelings and dreams to yourselves. That way, you avoid having too many people meddling in your business! Make every step toward your vows a commitment that strengthens the bond between the two of you.

Start with your family. Parents, grandparents, and siblings should receive the information first, preferably as a request for their blessing. Next, tell your closest friends, followed by people you intend to invite to your wedding. Leave your coworkers to as close to the wedding as possible, save for your office confidantes who should be discreet about your news.

MAKING THE ANNOUNCEMENT

The formal announcement of a couple's intention to marry is a way of informing the larger community. African tradition calls for family members, often females, to go through the village announcing to everyone that two of its residents are to become one. When two people come from different villages or cities, a public declaration would be made in each hometown.

In America, couples sometimes announce their engagement through the local newspaper and often have an engagement party or other announcement event. Many couples keep their news more private, telling only their loved ones.

In the Catholic church, it is required that the engagement be "posted," announced to the public three weeks prior to the wedding (this is called "posting the banns"). This is done to determine if anyone should see reason why the wedding should not take place.

Find out if your religion has requirements or restrictions regarding your announcement. If not, err on the side of discretion. Yes, you can post a public announcement in your newspaper with your photograph. It's best to do this close to the date of your wedding or after, as an acknowledgment that you married. In this way, all can share the joy.

Embracing Your Heritage

*A*S FAR BACK as the sixties the Black community began to emphasize the importance and validity of claiming its African heritage. Clusters of Black folks emerged, sharing their knowledge and understanding of the ways of ancestors. Even the most conservative Blacks began to consider how their own family background had affected their lives in an uplifting way. Credit for this emerging awareness came from several sources: The Black Power movement made everyone more aware of the strength to be found in our heritage; the Black church continued to espouse age-old wisdom about our resilience to all who entered its sanctuaries; and the media began to reflect more accurate images of who we were as a culture. The vibrations of spoken word wisdom passed down from generation to generation by our preachers, as well as by our ancestors, have found their way to us today.

We can and do find strength from the ways of old. Whether we look all the way back to the Motherland to discover spiritual rituals, styles of dress, or ways of communicating between families, or if we go just as far back as our family history will guide us, the look back is worth it. The Akan people of Ghana's Sankofa symbol comes to mind: The Sankofa symbol is most traditionally illustrated as a bird standing with feet forward and neck twisted around behind. In the bird's beak is an egg, representing the essence of its culture. In the Akan alphabet, Sankofa stands as a symbol harking us to "go back and fetch it." The broader understanding of this symbol is that it is our duty in life to stop in our tracks, turn, and look back at our lives and our history; claim the essence of who we are based on that history; and then turn and walk with grace, strength, and power into the present and the future.

Like the bird, there are moments when we can claim the legacy of who we are. One of these comes when people plan to marry, because a marriage is a union that brings more than two people together. Indeed, in West African tradition as well as in many indigenous cultures around the world, a marriage is considered a union of two families, which include at least two traditions, even when both families come from the same ethnic background. As you talk with your fiancé(e) and learn about each other's value systems, beliefs, and idiosyncrasies, you will reveal truths about yourselves that are worthy of inclusion in your wedding.

Take the time to reflect on who you are, the person you have become today, the person who is part of a dynamic familial and cultural heritage. Including the aspects of your background that define and support you makes your wedding unique.

❖ How to Claim Your Heritage

Where do you begin when practicing Sankofa? If you consider the period of your engagement as an actual part of your wedding, as so many of our African brothers and sisters still do today, you will be able to participate in this journey of exploration with greater ease. Don't think of this as a daunting task, but more as a process of revelation. Your journey to learn about your heritage and that of your partner can be deeply rewarding.

◆ Schedule time to visit your family elders. Start with your parents, aunts, and uncles. Talk to them about what they remember about your family. Ask them to tell you stories about the people who have long since passed. Ask for details about marriages in the family that have been successful

• • • • • • • • • •

as well as those that have not. Encourage them to be open in their sharing because you are interested in learning how to strengthen your marriage. Every piece of information can be useful.

- When you talk to your parents, ask them about how they came to give you your name. What significance does your name have to your life today—in their eyes? Compare you as a child to you as an adult. What is their perspective of you as a person about to be wed? What advice do they have for you on how to have a successful marriage? (This line of questioning is important even if your parents did not have a successful marriage. In either case, they will have ideas based on their knowledge of you and their understanding of what the marriage commitment means.)

- After you've gotten a sense of your family history from others, visit your grandparents if you are fortunate enough to have them alive, and ask them about specific people. Pay attention as their stories unfold. Ask about details of wedding ceremonies, personal styles, and characteristics of your family members. Also, ask for advice on how to be a good marriage partner.

- Go through family photo albums, and ask questions about the people you see. Don't pass a photo when you don't recognize a face; ask questions. Digging into your family legacy may not come easily at first; some stories seem better left untold. Be gentle but probing. Every story will reveal

- - - - - - - - - - -

something of value to you, even if you don't directly incorporate it into your wedding.

- Record all of these discussions on audio or videotape. If you
make a videotape, you may want to edit the interviews and
include them in your wedding ceremony. Imagine how surprised and pleased your guests will be to see and hear snip-
pets of your loved ones' memories in the midst of your
wedding!

- For the bride, ask your female elders, such as your mother
and your fiancé's mother, to participate in a gathering of
women sharing wisdom. As many of our African forebears
have done, invite these women to talk about their marriages
and the lessons they have learned. Listen for stories about
womenfolk of courage and sensuality. Inquire about how
they have made themselves alluring for their partners over
the years. Find out secrets they have for weathering storms.
Ask about the art of compromise. Listen and learn from
their stories.

- For the groom, invite your male elders and those of your fiancée to gather and share their wisdom. So often men are
not invited to speak up at family functions; here's their
chance. Tell the men that you want to learn how to be a
good husband. Ask for advice on being a partner, learning
to compromise, and details on how they have managed
through prickly situations in the past as well as stories from
other family members who may not be present or who may

have passed on. Inquire about forgiveness and faithfulness and how they have navigated these two great challenges in marriage. Listen and learn from their stories.

◆ Read up on your history. It can be easy now when you are able to surf the Internet, but don't stop there. Go to the library and inquire about wedding stories from this country, the Caribbean, and African countries. As you uncover bits of wisdom from other sources and times gone by, consider how some of them may be relevant to you today.

◆ Conduct research at your local African-American museum, a local university, or with historians who specialize in African-centered studies.

◆ Write your findings in your journal. You can incorporate your observations and insights into your wedding ceremony.

❖ Invoking the Ancestors

Talking to your family members and learning about times and people gone by can be very inspiring; the stories bring images to life that can fill you with warmth and happiness as well as pride. But don't stop there. Invoke those who have passed who will embrace your union if you welcome them.

There was a moment during my wedding that I will never forget. Theoretically, I understood that if you invoke the ancestors at a sacred ceremony, they will indeed come to support

· · · · · · · · · ·

you, and I very proudly share this wisdom with couples all over the country: "Remember the wise ones who are part of your own family heritage. Bring their memory to your ceremony. Call upon them to bless your union. Request them and they will come." But I had not actually experienced it firsthand—that is, until my wedding. The person who most influenced my life as a young person, besides my parents, was my maternal grandmother, whom we called Little Grandma. This small yet powerful woman exuded love and faith. She taught us through her actions how to treat others with respect and stand up for what we believed. She passed away not long before I met George. Though they didn't physically meet, he has met her in countless ways through my stories of her life and our interactions.

At our wedding, George and I incorporated a host of rituals and activities that represented our combined beliefs; among them was jumping the broom. We chose to jump at the conclusion of our ceremony, as a way to begin the recessional. Our minister, Dr. Eugene Callender, performed his role beautifully. He described in detail how our ancestors in this country had not been afforded the legal right to marry, even as they were encouraged to make family. To acknowledge and honor their unions they crafted a simple celebration that included jumping over a household broom. In an effort to make the event festive, the women commonly decorated the broom with flowers and fabric, and before the couple jumped, the men in the gathering would begin to drum, building up to a powerful crescendo. The music, vibration, and language of the drums would invoke the presence and grace of the ancestors. Come. Come. Be with us on this auspicious occasion. Bless us with your presence and your love.

The drum pulsed at our wedding, and we waited, holding hands, gazing into each other's eyes until the moment that we felt the drums cross the crescendo point. Then we looked forward and jumped. Although our jump could have lasted only a few moments and must have been only a few inches high in the air, our experience was that we were suspended in time. As I was air-bound, I saw what our African forebears had promised. There, just ahead of me, at the edge of the tent under which we were married, in the mist of the light rain that had begun to fall just as the drums began to beat, was Little Grandma. I could see her smiling, glowing face. Her approving smile. She had come to bless our union.

Yes, the wisdom of our African heritage is real. Believe it.

So, what can you do to invoke your ancestors? The most traditional means is through drumming. If you are interested in incorporating drumming into your wedding ceremony, be sure to check with your officiant. Weddings in spiritual sanctuaries often have restrictions on what musical instruments are allowed. While some accommodate drums, others do not. If you are allowed to have drumming, find professional drummers and listen to them play. Talk to them about where in your ceremony you want to invoke your ancestors; the choices vary widely.

. . . .

Some couples choose to open the ceremony with drumming music, incense, and African dancers—before the bride enters. Others wait to grow the spiritual energy until just before or after the vows are declared. At the moment when you are actually committing to one another, inviting your ancestors to join you can be tremendously moving. Still others wait and continue their actual wedding ceremony at their reception site, where they jump the broom to the beat of the drum, signaling part two of their joining. Some use drumming music when no drummers are there to be found. As you craft your ceremony, you can choose.

Blending African and African-American Traditions: The Wedding of Hatshepsut and Richard Symister

In a way, our ceremony started one year before we got married. We both follow the Khamitic teachings of the Husia, the oldest written spiritual document known to humans, which lays down a spiritual path by which we should live.

Richard proposed on the beach in Ocho Rios, Jamaica, where his father, now an ancestor, was born. Of course, I accepted.

A week before our public ceremony that involved the "village" (our family and friends), we had a private ceremony with two of the elders in our spiritual community: Baba Kham, of Oasis at Sunrise, and his wife, Queen Mother Mut Ast. We began our sacred day by awaking at four o'clock in the morning and purifying ourselves. After that, we both clothed ourselves and wrapped our heads in white.

When we arrived at the temple, we were asked a series of questions to de-

termine if we were up to the task and responsibility of marriage and if we understood our obligation to the community. After answering the questions, we were given permission by our spiritual elders to jump over the ankh and "cross over" together. We were each given our own ankh, which we wore on our left arms. We then gave each other a greeting of recognition as spiritual husband and wife, and reaffirmed our plan to include our village in a public ceremony.

A week later we held our public ceremony at the Blairhaven Retreat Center in Duxbury, Massachusetts. We awoke at sunrise and expressed our thanks to the "four corners": north, south, east and west. At the ceremony, we wanted to include as many Caribbean elements as possible to honor and recognize the sustenance of African culture in those lands, as well as here. Our colors were yellow, turquoise, coral/orange and brown with ivory as an accent color, representing Oshun, the spiritual guardian of love and beauty. Although this is in the Yoruba tradition, most African traditions have a spiritual parallel. In using these colors, we also represented many of the Khamitic guardians. Our ceremony space was decorated in pink, the color of Maat, draped in white, and accented with gold. These colors represent coming forth; a kind of graduation.

Our guests were greeted by a steel pannist playing traditional calypso music. Our wedding party and the groom's party marched in to "I Don't Want to Wait in Vain," by Bob Marley; I marched in to "Is This Love That I'm Feeling," also by Bob Marley. Both my parents walked me down the aisle because, in the Khamitic tradition, there must be a balance of both male and female energy.

We took a moment to acknowledge that in the waters of Kingston Bay slave ships had dropped many of "us" off in the Caribbean. We recognized

• • • • • • • • • •

and honored those ancestors that died on that soil, and invited them and our personal ancestors to be with us. After that, the community was told of its duty to us. We professed what our responsibility to each other and the community was and promised to hold one another's life's work.

At a small table we were given salt, for sustaining life; wine, for mixing of the blood of families; pepper, to remember that there would be heated times; water, to purify; bitter herbs, to remember the hard times; a spoon and wooden bowl, to remember to nourish each other; a shield, to protect the home; a spear, to defend it; and finally a broom, to remember to keep order in the house. We held the broom and together swept the altar space, demonstrating to the community our willingness to bring order to our marriage and the community. We then placed the broom in front of the altar, and jumped over it.

Our recessional was "One Love," by Bob Marley. We invited everyone to a tent overlooking the water and had a Karamu, or feast, to celebrate our union.

❖ Claiming Your Ancestors

Take time to identify precisely which ancestors you want to invoke. In West African tradition, families keep memories alive of those who lived honorable lives, whose lives are worthy of remembering. By keeping the flame of their legacy alive, the villagers breathe inspiration and focus into all who live now.

In the same way, you can recall your own families and communities. Who are the people who meant the most to you when you were growing up who have since passed on? Whose marriages do you remember as great examples to follow? Be specific in your recollections. Don't worry if your thoughts take you outside your nuclear family into the heart of your community; from an African perspective, your community *is* your family. Who stands out in your life today as an example that you respect? As you come up with individuals who have either directly affected you or whose stories you have grown to know and love, jot them down. When you and your fiancé meet to talk about your planning progress, discuss your ancestors. Refer back to the questions you asked your family members, and recall stories of those wise ones whom they revere as well. Determine who is important to each of you and how you choose to honor them in your wedding.

Lighting a Candle

When record executive Derek Angelettie and his fiancée, Lisa Miller, got married in New Jersey, their parents stood at their sides while their grandparents and other family elders who had passed on stood with them symbolically. The couple decided to invoke these ancestors in their wedding with a ritual lighting of a unity candle. While the two of them lit the center candle, each of their mothers lit a candle on the side. As they lit the candles, each mother called out the names of family members who had passed on whom they wanted to be present for this momentous occasion. During the candle-lighting ceremony, the guests gathered remained silent. All you could hear were the quivering voices of these two mothers calling out their loved ones' names.

Holding a Seat

One of the most important people in Jocelyn Cooper's life was her father. Andrew Cooper and his bride of fifty-four years, Jocelyn, Sr., had enjoyed a close and loving relationship with each of their daughters. Despite his illness, Andrew Cooper spent quality time with Jocelyn's intended, Christopher Halliburton, and gave his blessing for their marriage before he passed. Indeed, it was the last thing that her father said to Jocelyn before he died. At Jocelyn's fall wedding, just six months after her father's death, the family decided to reserve a chair on the front row next to Mrs. Cooper, where they placed the program from his funeral and a flower. In the family's mind's eye, Dad was surely present.

During the wedding ceremony itself, the officiant offered a special blessing in honor of both Jocelyn's father, Andrew Cooper, and Christopher's father, Norman Halliburton, Sr., both of whom had passed.

What You Can Do

Let your creativity and your memories of loved ones guide your decisions about how to include your ancestors in your wedding. Here are a few suggestions from other couples that may spark your creative ideas:

. . . .

- Invite family elders who are mobile to come to the altar and light a candle for each ancestor. Make sure you have enough candles and that they are beautifully arranged. Long matches make the actual lighting elegant.
- Write an acknowledgment of your ancestors in your program.
- Ask the officiant to make a prayer of remembrance for them.
- Include framed photographs of significant ancestors on your wedding altar.
- Hire drummers to offer a drum invocation of the ancestors.
- Hire dancers to enact a remembrance ritual of the ancestors that also illustrates the joining of the two families.
- Ask your officiant to offer blessings to the four directions—East, South, West, and North—to welcome and acknowledge the energy of the ancestral spirits and ask for their blessings. This is a Cherokee ritual; indigenous people all over the world have similar rituals.

❖ Honoring Your Elders

At this great family affair, your elders from both families deserve a place of honor. When crafting your sacred ceremony, consider who among your elders you want to include and in what fashion. When you think of the wedding in the context of more than one day, your decision may be easier; you can plan small events leading up to your big day that include elders in appropriate ways. Just as our African ancestors often did, you can stage gatherings where the women gather with the women and the men with the men for the purpose of sharing knowledge and support. Among the Islamic Rashaida nomads of Egypt and the Sudan, for example, weddings last about a week. On the first evening, after the couple is officially married and receive the blessings of the holy man and the community, an exclusive gathering of men occurs during which the men give the groom money and they celebrate with food and drink. The bride, meanwhile, is sequestered in a private tent where she keeps company with her mother and sisters.

What can you do? If you have a great-aunt who is homebound, why not take a small contingent of female family members and friends to her home to celebrate? Bring food and beverages and gifts—including items that she will be able to recognize as meaningful to your relationship with her. During your visit, express your intentions about marrying and ask for her wisdom. Have all the women gathered participate in a round-robin, sharing stories of hope and memory about the beauty and promise of partnership. The groom can do the same with male elders.

Beyond those who are physically old are the members of your family who are simply older than you. This includes your parents, aunts and uncles, and others who have become family who hold a place of reverence in your life. Remember them when you plan your event, and share your plans for their participation.

Here are ideas for what you can do for your elders:

♦ Seat family elders together in reserved pews or seating areas. During the ceremony, have your officiant invite them to stand with your parents as a symbol of the families joining as one. The order that the officiant can call people to stand might be as follows: parents, grandparents, aunts and uncles, any additional family elders, siblings, and then the rest of the congregation.

♦ Write a special message to the elders in your program that you have someone read during the ceremony in the midst of other readings.

♦ Offer gifts to your family elders during the ceremony; they can be placed on or near the altar. When the family is acknowledged, the two of you can hand them to each family elder. If you do this, be sure to have a few extras in case someone you didn't remember shows up!

♦ Make sure that the typeface on the programs is large, or consider having separate programs printed for elders. If you do this, be sure to make them as beautiful as the others. I highly recommend that you print more than you imagine you need.

♦ Check to see where the restrooms are at your ceremony and reception site. Too often the flow of an event can be

. . . .

compromised because a disabled or slower-moving guest cannot get to or from the facilities in time to experience or participate in the event.

◆ Assign compassionate family members or friends to watch over your elders. Be mindful as you select attendants to be sure that they are well suited for the task. When George and I got married, our friend Vimilakshi Archer instinctively stepped in to fulfill this duty. Our aunts and George's grandmother were so independent that it hadn't occurred to us that anyone would need an arm to lean on. We got married in a Japanese tea garden that was beautiful, but the pathways were narrow; there were pebbles here and there and not many handrails. Vimilakshi accompanied my aunt Audrey in particular throughout the day. Aunt Audrey was supported without being made to feel disabled or old. Instead, she just felt loved.

❖ Lessons We Can Learn from the Motherland

We talk a lot about the practices of our ancestors that we choose to embrace and call our own, yet few couples today welcome being part of an arranged marriage, even though they still occur in African culture—as well as in many other cultures—today, though this is not a common practice for African Americans.

Malidoma Some describes the marriage rites in his village of Burkina Faso, West Africa, in his book *Of Water and the Spirit*.

* * * * * * * * * * *

There, the male elders who hold the vision of the community and understand people's roles within it can see who is properly suited for whom.

In addition to spiritual compatibility, economics and social stability have often ranked high on the list of qualities considered in other cultures. When family members conduct background checks to find out if two people might be properly suited, their financial stability and family reputation are important factors. Many believe that to create a strong family unit, you must start with two people who are compatible family- and value-wise, which usually requires that both come from the same social and economic group.

Today in America, we experience the greatest amount of freedom available in the world. Whereas Black folks once were lynched for even looking at a White person, we now have the legal right to marry anyone we choose—of any race, economic background, religion, or country. So how do you find a partner who is well-suited for you when your family and community are often absent from selecting your life partner? More objective and concerned eyes might discover truths about the two lovebirds that each was incapable of noticing about the other.

This is why it is so important to seek out the blessing of your family members *before* you seal your deal. Even if you are older, it is still wise to build a bond between your parents and other kinfolk and your intended. Schedule family meetings over the course of your engagement. Make time to get to know each other. Be open with your parents in your discussions about your plans. Of course, you want to maintain a certain level of privacy, but if you approach your parents and confidantes as allies who want the best for you, your discourse can be rewarding.

Marriage, when considered as a lifetime commitment, deserves all the support it can get from the beginning. Both your families can provide insights into the other person and the ways in which you and your families have looked at life. And do note that when your family members bring up the touchy subjects of religion, money, and class, if you and your fiancé differ, take heed. Yes, it's possible to overcome any obstacle before you if your commitment is strong enough. But know that the fundamental ways in which you view the world, often having to do with your spiritual beliefs and your economic outlook and values, are hard to change. Look at these aspects of your life candidly and soberly. Talk about them openly. There's no brushing them or any other points of contention under the rug. Any conflicts that are left unaddressed will rise up at some point. Bring them up now so that you can work through whatever stands in the way of your creating a loving and lasting union.

The Value of Marriage

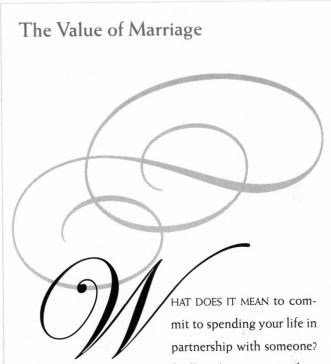

W HAT DOES IT MEAN to commit to spending your life in partnership with someone? In contemporary culture, with all its distractions and attractions, what does the promise of marriage mean? In the life that you are building with your beloved, what do you believe you are vowing to do?

These thought-provoking questions will either resonate in your minds and hearts as you take steps toward the sacred altar, or you will fill your time with other activities, all the while ignoring the voice inside that is calling you to declare your commitment. I urge you to heed the call from within. That your heart has opened so fully to be ready to welcome another person means that you are ready to look within for the vision of your life together. True, you cannot predict the future. No one can. Yet your heart holds answers about the measure and depth of your commitment to the one you have grown to love, appreciate, and respect. Devote the time it takes to discover how your heart describes your feelings and the meaning of your bond. Figure out before you physically "get married" what you believe the value of marriage is for the two of you.

When George and I decided to marry, I knew it was my duty to consider the commitment seriously. I had been married previously; George had not. Having suffered through a painful divorce, I knew that I needed to be clear and precise about what my expectations and needs were in marriage before entering into it again. I knew that George was a great man. He even fit the description, which I had painted in my heart when I was a little girl, of who my husband would be. As an adult, though, I didn't believe that was enough. As I pondered the questions "What will our commitment mean over time?" and "Why do I want to marry him?" I continued to be actively involved in my spiritual life. Working on strengthening me from the inside out, I also explored how one can do that inner work while walking alongside a partner, and gained a priceless piece of wisdom: *Marriage is partnership in spiritual practice.* My own spiritual journey already had shown me that working on your own life and seeking God's love and support are worth it even as the work can sometimes be ex-

. . . .

cruciatingly difficult. Could it be that marriage would be like that too? As I have talked to married couples who have lived through many ups and downs, it has become clear that in marriage you experience all of the emotions, challenges, defeats, and victories that life brings your way. When you anchor your union in the understanding that you will have a loving partner at your side on your spiritual journey, you can experience strength and comfort throughout your life, no matter what comes your way. M. Scott Peck, author of *The Road Less Traveled,* an amazing guidebook to the pursuit of spiritual truth, also wrote *A World Waiting to Be Born.* In this book he says, and I agree, that "a marriage properly should be a marriage of two people gathered together for some purpose higher than the mere pleasure of being together: namely, to enhance each other's spiritual journeys." He also says that apart from the desire to have and care for children, the only other valid reason for getting married "is for the friction." Friction in the context of spiritual growth represents a profound stimulus for one's life, doesn't it?

This is a powerful truth about choice and intention. Marriage is a choice people can make with the understanding that they will be traveling together on a spiritual journey. Every moment presents an opportunity for choice. One emotion or situation may call you this way, while another beckons you in the opposite direction. When you stand in the conviction and clarity that come from knowing your own heart, you can make choices wisely and choose to take steps that affirm the best in you. The choice of

. . . .

marriage—to the right partner—is one of those wise choices. It is up to you and your partner to define your life together. When you work on it before you actually marry, you stand a much better chance of starting off from a position of strength.

Included here are words of wisdom from others of all backgrounds who are married or have been. Voices of officiants and newlyweds, couples married more than half their lives and those recently divorced and widowed, share their personal wisdom here to inspire you to consider what you believe the value of marriage is and what you intend the commitment of marriage to be in your life. I trust that they will inspire you to discover what the bond of marriage means to you. You may consider incorporating some of their language into your vows or another part of your ceremony. You may simply choose to talk to your fiancé(e) about what you've learned or put into action some nugget of inspiration that resonates within you.

❖ Sacred and Civil

Wilbur Levin, the county clerk for Kings County in New York, who has been married for more than sixty years, crafted this statement, which he offers in all weddings that he performs. I think you will find that these words hold great power.

Marriage is a partnership, the most significant one either of you will ever enter. Partners are persons who work together toward a common goal, sharing the

benefits. The key word is share. *You will do just that the rest of your lives. As
we all know, life is full of surprises and the unforeseen. These try persons' souls
and strain relationships. Partners sometimes disagree on how to cope with demands that come their way. This is natural, to be expected, and I promise you
will occur. But you are about to promise me and pledge in this gathering of
family and friends that you will address your challenges together with common purpose, shoulder to shoulder resolve your differences, share the burdens,
and never, never abdicate your responsibilities to one another. In return, I
guarantee you happiness and a sense of loving, a comradeship that will exceed
your expectations; that your relationship will grow and flourish with each
passing year; that when your hair is gray, you will delight in each other's
company with even more fullness than you do today. I know where ere I speak.
That has been my experience, can be yours, and prayerfully will be.*

❖ Wisdom from the Elders

When Caroline Clarke and Johnny Graves got married after
dating for several years, they incorporated fun and loving guidance into their preparations. For Caroline, the wisdom came in
a surprising way. Her female friends threw her what she termed
"a raunchy bridal shower" that was followed by a "sweet prayer
breakfast" hosted by her mother, godmother, and aunts. Here's
how Caroline describes the event:

*They handed out these little prayer cards, and each wrote some bit of advice
for me on the back. Most of these women had been married twenty, thirty,
forty, and more years. Many of them have since passed on. I cherish these*

cards and their advice like you wouldn't believe. I have pulled out the scrap-book that contains their handwritten notes often over the years. I didn't real-ize at the time what a treasure they would be. Some of the best:

Never leave or meet each other without a kiss. —Olga Wiles (who sparked our first date)

Let go and let God. When it all looks like too much, laugh. *It will get better.* —Helene Cave

Forgive and forget! —Yvonne Jean Jacques

If a plan does not work, shift! And keep shifting until it does. —Gloria Wright

Always remember: When he gets on your nerves, pray for him. —Lucille Norville Perez

If you are angry, talk it out, don't act it out. —Vera Clarke (my mom)

Caroline explains that she has drawn on these treasured bits of wisdom over the years. For her, being in a lasting marriage es-sentially means this: Marriage matters. She says, "It's a commit-ment to be taken seriously and worked very hard at when necessary, which, I've discovered, means much of the time." Married since 1992, she has been successful at it thus far!

❖ Inspiring Declarations of Love

The wisest decision I've made in my life was made at a very young age: twenty-one. It was to marry my childhood sweetheart. We are members of the

same tribe that formed in a little neighborhood in southeast San Diego during the late thirties and early forties. That we've known each other most of our lives, that our families go back together more than sixty years, that we share common background, upbringing, and values has been the key factor in ensuring that our marriage has survived through the inevitable ups and downs that close relationships encounter over extended periods of time, thirty-five years in our case.

—Charles Ward, married to Cheryl Ward since 1968

My mother and Charles's mother were neighbors and they planned our marriage before we were born, so his mother says. I guess they knew we'd "mind" them and their great plan. I'm extremely grateful for their vision! Charles and I have an incredible history together that has made us more than husband and wife, we are indeed soul mates. Our friendship started when we were seven or eight and has seen us through the many challenges we all face in life, in love, in marriage. I think being friends is critical in a relationship, and he's my best. The "historic memory" that we share through growing up together is a connection we cherish, and it is heightened by our large extended families, our experiences together, our personal joys and sorrows. We're proud of each other, our families, and our long-lasting relationship and hope it's a good example for others, just as our elders have been examples to us. Besides all that, he's a great dad and a great storyteller, he makes me laugh a lot, and he cleans the kitchen better than I do. I pray we have another thirty-five years together.

—Cheryl Ward, married to Charles Ward since 1968

Let nothing come between you and your vows—your mama, your business, your dog, your children, your minister, nothing, and nobody. The moment

you do it undermines the sacred bond you've made. . . . If you allow anything to come between you, know that you are distancing yourself from each other. Everybody wants to give you advice. It's like having a baby. Everybody wants to tell you how to have it, but nobody can tell you how to get it.
—Peggy Dillard Toone, married to Lloyd Toone since 1980

The interesting thing about marriage for me has been that I've taken on the life of another person and incorporated that life into my own. Whatever I do or say, the other person has to be considered.

   What one would like to do is to develop the kind of relationship in which two people are so harmonious and in sync together, in which their love is so strong, that they become one individual again. You have to let go of all your fears, hang-ups, preconceived notions of what a marriage is or should be. The one becomes two, and then the two become one: that's the ultimate goal. Within that unity, you still have your own distinct personalities, but you function as a couple, as one. This is something to strive for—it doesn't just happen. But when you reach that point, it's the ultimate, because that's true love. That love supersedes jealousy and all of that, because you believe this person is as totally committed to you as you are to her, and the love frees you to the point that there's total trust and understanding and communication beyond words.
—Lloyd Toone, married to Peggy Dillard Toone since 1980

What marriage means to me is making a commitment to someone with whom you plan to spend the rest of your life, understanding that this commitment will change over time. That you are willing to become and remain best friends, first and foremost, lovers in early years, sensual partners in later years, al-

· · · · · · · · · ·

ways being ready to admit a mistake and being able to forgive your partner and yourself, and finally loving and having faith in each other.

—Janice Carter, married to Dwight Carter since 1977

I believe that the love in marriage is one that you refresh every day. Every moment it is my duty and privilege to demonstrate my love to my wife, and this is what I do. I don't make too many moves in my day without thinking about my wife. My world is made up of how I feel about my wife every day. Out of this love comes a tremendous amount of strength for me personally and in my marriage.

—Dwight Carter, married to Janice Carter since 1977

You can stand up in front of the church and say these vows, but I don't know if they necessarily mean that much until you make a personal commitment to yourself and you decide that this really is your life partner, that's when the vows really kick in. It took me a couple of years before I committed me to me. . . .

One thing that's especially important to me is having a person who is my friend, my lover, my wife, my children's mother, who is with me wholeheartedly and 100 percent, no matter what. A person who knows she can look at me and see how I'm feeling and hug me and say, "Let's talk" . . . Having a person who is unequivocally with you that you don't have to question has been very important through all our trials and tribulations. Knowing that she's in my corner is very important to me.

—John Pinderhughes, married to Victoria Pinderhughes since 1982

. . . .

Going into a marriage takes a certain amount of risk because you don't know what the path will be like, but there's enough that you find appealing, compatible, interesting in that person to take the chance to find out. Over the course of the marriage you have to work at it to hold onto the good things that got you into the relationship and maintain that and help it to thrive. . . . We are a team: the good stuff, the bad stuff, the rocky stuff. We are in this together, and that was part of the original vow: for better, for worse and for richer, for poorer. I would never say obey, *because I felt we had to be equals, full partners. . . . We work a lot better than we did in the beginning: Disagreements get resolved more quickly; we can laugh a little more readily at some things that would have been like World War III many years ago. I realize that no relationship is perfect, and there are so many good things in our relationship that make it worth fighting for and keeping and continuing. The longer you're together, the more comfortable you get. It's familiar. It's a good thing. I still love this man.*
—Victoria Pinderhughes, married to John Pinderhughes since 1982

The value of our marriage is incalculable, for both of us. By knowing me, she lets me experience and understand what she knows—and vice versa. She is strong where I am weak, and her weaknesses allow me to be strong for her. She is exquisite in body and soul, and isn't life fullest when lived surrounded by beauty?
—Richard Marek, married to Dalma Heyn since 1991

Throughout our marriage, my husband and I have noticed that many childhood hurts and vulnerabilities have become less sore, less raw. It's as if certain

• • • • • • • • • •

deep parts of us, once ragged around the edges, have slowly mended. Psychology calls this a "corrective" emotional experience—and it is. To have the power literally to heal each other is one of the profoundest effects of commitment.

—Dalma Heyn, married to Richard Marek since 1991

Marriage offers the stability to your personal life and to your work that allows you to concentrate on what's truly important in life, leaving the distractions behind.

—Oz Scott, married to Lynne Scott since 1978

Marriage is a wonderful experience provided you are involved with someone you not only know, but indeed connect with beyond mental and physical bases. Once that line has been crossed and you're both sure you want to settle down, then embracing her [or him] as part of your life can certainly only make you stronger. I think, with this in place, the commitment comes naturally.

—Daryl Pendana, married to Sharon Pendana since 1998

Marriage is beautiful. Not Hollywood-ending prettiness, but rather the messy mix of in-spite-of as well as because-of beauty. We enjoy blissful highs, survive abysmal lows, and we endure. We love, "warts and all." In marriage, we have to surrender, and in those sacrifices we gain so much more. Becoming less me-focused and more we-focused is a natural process of marriage. And in this process, we grow. We are humbled in the experience, yet enriched by it. I truly believe that in honoring our partners and our commitment

• • • • • • • • • •

to marriage, we mature and equip ourselves with the tools to live in harmony with humanity at large, and thus our surrender to the marital "we" enhances our dealing with the communal "we."

Commitment in marriage at its best is the unerring quest to nurture the joined lives of two as one. It is honoring the sanctity of union by respecting its sacred nature. True commitment makes us access "the better angels of our nature." When we see the divine in our partners, we want to reflect that divinity and reach ever higher in truth, respect, fidelity, sharing, perseverance, and always, love.

—Sharon Pendana, married to Daryl Pendana since 1998

My marriage to Jason is a castle, a place where I can luxuriate in being simply myself. So often, the lingo of marriage refers to the fact that it is something you build—which is true. I strive to be loving, kind, patient, to not take him or our love for granted. But it's an incredible feeling to know that someone has made a place for you in his life, where you are welcome whether you've lost ten pounds or gained twenty, whether you're having a bad hair day or a bad attitude week. The reason I married Jason, the reason I know that I am incredibly blessed, is that at the very heart of our marriage, there is this castle, this structure of love and support, that is always there and where I am always welcome.

—Veronica Chambers, married to Jason Clampet since 2002

When Stephanie and I got married it was the second marriage for me. So I wasn't thinking about getting married again. Stephanie said, "Let's just have fun." I thought about that and I thought that was a good reason to do it; it *would make her very happy to go through life married. This reason was fine. I didn't want anything heavy or difficult. My last marriage was heavy and difficult. . . . It was enough for me to go through my life with someone who wants to have fun and to be happy.*

I found out after all of these years that anytime we ran into difficulties and we tried to figure out what the problem was, it was that we weren't having fun. So we would go to the islands or go to the movies. There is always something fun to do. When we get jammed, we try to find fun, and when we do, we're back on track.

—Reginald Oliver, married to Stephanie Stokes Oliver since 1979

The value of marriage is the establishment of family. When you first date the person, you're having fun and you do get companionship, which is a long-term benefit of marriage. But over time you discover that you have established family with him, his family, any children you may have together or separately, and the relatives. After a certain point, you discover that everyone accepts him and you as a part of the family. That's how families are made. I wanted to perpetuate family in that way, particularly since I had seen and lived with what I thought was a goal-model marriage through my parents. . . .

The commitment is the seed of the longevity and the commitment is the glue. I think we commit to lesser things all the time—opening a bank account at the bank, with a mortgage company, going to a certain college, to jobs and careers, to our church. So, to me, it was just a natural thing to make a commitment to a person and it really saddens me to see that [fewer] people are committing to [each other], particularly in the Black community. . . . It's not anything to be afraid of. It's something to celebrate, and it's part of being

* * * * * * * * * *

grown. . . . We should be more like the society of our African heritage that loves our children but reveres our elders.
—Stephanie Stokes Oliver, married to Reginald Oliver since 1979

The commitment of marriage lies in putting God first in the marriage, respecting your partner's opinions and ideas, faithfulness, and communication. What I value about marriage is that you take a spiritual journey through life, to life eternal together, raising children together, and praying with and for each other.
—Veronica Frazier, married to William Frazier since 1972

The commitment of marriage lies in being truthful to your partner in all things, never giving up even when times get rough, and trusting in the Lord. What I value about marriage is having the woman I chose as my wife beside me through all these years and to watch our boys grow into competent young men.
—William Frazier, married to Veronica Frazier since 1972

One often associates value with price. In the case of marriage, it is priceless, like the artistic works of the great masters. Together you must build a foundation, firmly rooted. It can never be taken for granted, but rather continuously maintained and nurtured by mutual respect, faith, and love.
—Frank Robinson, married to Nancy Robinson since 1953

Marriage is valuable for the creation of family, the foundation of our society. A ceremony and a signed certificate do not make a marriage. It takes commitment, along with a lot of "mutual respect, faith, and love" and hard work!
—Nancy Robinson, married to Frank Robinson since 1953

. . . .

I believe the value of marriage is priceless and the commitment of marriage is to give endlessly, following Christ's devotion that he gave for us.
—Ernest Johnson and Rashell-Lady Brundage-Johnson, *married since August 2002*

To us, marriage represents a love that is everlasting, a love that is as vital as air, as comforting as a gentle stroke, as comfortable as a Caribbean night, and stronger than any bond made by man. It must be each of these, for it is tested every day. That it endures is an expression of our commitment to each other, to our children, and to our God. To each of us, there is no greater joy than the blessings that have been born of our union, our marriage.
—Roy Johnson and Barbara Johnson, *married since 1991*

Marriage for us has meant that we know that we're together for us, and not to please other people. We are somewhat old-fashioned and really see marriage as something permanent, so it's something that says that we know we're in love, that we have an understanding, and that we're going to tough this out no matter what—even if other people think we've got other motives other than just wanting to have a life together.
—Alexandra Sanidad Zangrillo and Vincent Zangrillo, *married in 2002*

Having committed myself to Rick—amidst friends, family, and God—means I have given myself completely to him. As such, Rick provides the way for me to fully practice and learn what it means to be human. Our pledge to each other was to see God in one another. To love, respect, and honor one another as divine. Rick helps me remember my own greatness, and I, in turn, re-

. . . .

flect to him the wonder of who he is. When I forget and act from a small or contracted place out of fear or anger, inevitably I remember our promises and commitments to one another, and love flows once again. I consider myself fortunate beyond words to smooth out my rough edges because of my relationship with Rick.

—Shakti Butler, married to Rick Butler since 1988

I think the value of marriage is in the development of a lifelong partner, which also requires a lot of personal development that enhances the individual and also gives back to the partnership. The commitment of marriage means that I am not doing things from an educational point of view, not like a job, where you have an education to do a certain thing. Marriage is based on a belief, a belief in love, which is so intangible. Love is not a skill, like something you have for a job; once I recognized that, it became so comforting, eternally comforting.

—Zachary Minor, married to Wickham Boyle since 1995

The value of marriage is a balance that moves from calm vibration to a volatile safety—a sensation like knowing you can sail on the ocean. Marriage provides a base to have another person weather all the huge joys and travails of life but asks that you be really present. The commitment means that even when times are tough or you think the other person is a real dope, that you push yourself to find the magical essence that caused you to fall in love and make the commitment in the first place. Without marriage, one is free to slam the door and not return.

—Wickham Boyle, married to Zachary Minor since 1995

Marriage gives two people the opportunity to learn to live together in mutual understanding of each other's fallibility. And to be able to love one another in spite of whatever their shortcomings might be.

Marriage gives us an opportunity to bring new life into the world and to be able to watch these lives grow and develop and give them space to make their own decisions, though we as parents might want to protect them too much and thereby keep them from growing as much as they possibly can grow. It brings us together as a family unit. Just think of what you've been able to create. It's just a wonderful, wonderful thing, particularly when you are growing right along with your children and being able to understand their needs and meet them as much as you are possibly able to meet them and create a loving, warm cocoon in which they can live and develop. But just as the butterfly comes out of the cocoon, the children start to emerge and start the circle anew. . . .

From the vantage point of being a widow, I never conceived of the idea that I would ever be alone. It never crossed my mind, and it just points up to you how dependent you become on your spouse, and no matter how independent you have been, either one of you, if one leaves the other behind, there's just a void. Though we don't in our lifetimes dwell on the fact that we are not always going to be here together, knowing this now, I believe we should learn to cherish each day that we have together and work to make it the best day that it can be for all of us.

—Doris Cole, married to Harry Cole for forty-one years before he passed

Elements of Your Sacred Ceremony

*I*NVOKING GRACE into your wedding ceremony is a powerful way of beginning your married life. *How* you choose to welcome the sacred into your union is what you must decide. Your beliefs, values, and commitment will determine the specific elements that will become part of your wedding ceremony. If you intend to marry as part of a spiritual tradition, you will find that many defining elements already exist, but even so, you can work with your officiant to tailor certain details to your liking. If you are having an interfaith ceremony, you will need to make a number of decisions, starting with whether you want one or more officiants to preside over your wedding and where it will occur. If you decide to host your wedding in a neutral location with an open-minded officiant who is willing to work with you to create a unique ceremony, it's time for you to let your creativity come to the forefront.

❖ Ambiance

The ambiance at a wedding is important. From the moment that guests approach the site, they should feel that they are going to be part of a joyous and sacred experience. Every detail counts in designing the space that will hold the sacred energy of your wedding. For this reason, it is wise for the two of you and your wedding coordinator or site coordinator to visit the wedding ceremony site several times, preferably at the time of day when you intend to have your wedding. Notice your surroundings:

- What do the grounds look like as you approach? Is there any debris that needs to be cleared away? Are there any outdoor vases where you can place flowers?

- How do you feel as you walk through the entrance? Does the energy change as you go from outside to inside? If you are getting married under a tent, request to see sample tents to be sure that they don't have a musty smell and that they give a grand or an intimate feeling, depending on your desire.

- What does the space smell like when you enter? Some

churches or older venues may not smell fresh. For both sacred and aesthetic reasons, many couples choose to burn incense in the sanctuary at least an hour before the service begins. You will have to check with the officiant to see if this is permitted.

* What features of the ceremony site stand out as supportive of the mood you want to set? How can you play them up? For example, if an ornately beautiful chandelier hangs near the entryway of the church, you can place a simply designed table underneath, on which are the guest sign-in book and programs. An attendant can stand nearby to welcome guests as they arrive.

* Does the altar or the location where you will create an altar represent your vision? You may want to add flowers or candles to soften or elevate the mood of the space.

* What else can you add that will bring the space to life?

❖ The Fragrance of Flowers

Our brothers and sisters in the Caribbean usually have only to host their wedding outdoors in order to have the best of everything. Exotic tropical flowers bloom plentifully in Jamaica, Barbados, the Bahamas, and throughout much of the rest of the Caribbean. Many of these flowers have hypnotic fragrances matched only by their breathtaking beauty.

But what if you're not getting married on a tropical island?

· · · · · · · · · · ·

If you live in a big city, you have access to just about everything—for a price.

When you search for the right flowers, have a clear sense of the theme of your wedding so that you don't get overwhelmed by the choices. What colors will you and your fiancé wear? What complementary colors will your bridal party wear? What colors will you use as accents to design the spaces around you—at both the ceremony and reception?

Armed with that information, visit a florist. First, *smell* the flowers. In the spirit of invoking the sacred, I strongly recommend that you select your flowers based primarily on fragrance, and on appearance second. They can be combined with blooms that have a strong visual appeal but a neutral or no fragrance. No matter how small or big your budget, remember the importance of the day and make each flower count, from the bride's bouquet to the boutonniere.

Here is a listing of some of the most fragrant and romantic flowers, combined with flowers that have visual appeal and a neutral scent:

AROMATIC VARIETIES

- Casablanca lily
- Lily of the valley
- Gardenia
- Roses of all varieties, especially
  the pink rose and the silver dollar

- Night-blooming jasmine
- Hyacinth
- Freesia
- Narcissus

VISUALLY BEAUTIFUL: Not Necessarily Fragrant

- Calla lily
- Bougainvillea
- Hibiscus
- Bird of paradise
- Dendrobium orchid
- Peony
- Magnolia
- Stephanotis
- Iris
- Delphinium
- Hydrangeas
- Queen Anne's lace

❖ The Magic of Music

What music will define your wedding? How will you use music to create a sacred environment in which everyone will be drawn to focus on the event at hand? The sound of soothing and inviting music can waft through the air to a guest's car. When the door opens, the guest is greeted with the voice of welcome that music can provide.

First you must figure out where your musical tastes and those of your partner match up. You also must learn if there are musical requirements or restrictions at your ceremony site. In some spiritual sanctuaries, you are allowed to play only music that is approved by the house of worship. In that case, you should meet with the musical director to find out what your choices are and listen to a sampling of them played by the musicians who are allowed to play at your wedding. If the house of worship allows you to hire your own musicians, find out how innovative the musicians can get. For example, a classical piece played by a jazz saxophonist can invoke a completely different mood than one played on a pipe organ. If you are not limited in the style or selection of music, you can give your imagination and individuality free rein.

Generally, there are several musical periods during a wedding: the prelude, the processional, and the recessional, and sometimes vocal selections during the ceremony.

Prelude

Select soothing music that invites guests to be still as they enter your sacred space. Classical music, jazz, or other instrumental music that is quiet and introspective are good choices.

Processional

Here, you can use three different musical selections. The first piece of music signals the congregation that your wedding is about to begin and is used as the music to which the mothers of the groom and the bride are brought to their respective seats. This piece can be joyous and uplifting, with a lively step. The mothers should be escorted by one of the ushers, their husbands, or another family member who serves as an usher. If the father of the bride will be escorting her to her groom, he should not be the escort for his wife. If the mother of the bride is remarried, her husband can escort her to her seat and then sit where it has been agreed he will sit, either next to her, leaving space closest to the aisle for the bride's father, or in the pew or row behind his wife.

The next selection is for the bridal party. The bridesmaids will walk up the aisle either individually or accompanied by a groomsman. This music can also be lively and joyous and it's best for it to be instrumental. The bridal party should take their places, framing the space for the bride and groom.

Next comes the music that introduces the bride. Usually the flower girl precedes the bride and her escort, walking to the bride's music, creating a dramatic entrance for the bride. This music can be a spiritual melody, a classical composition, or a contemporary song that speaks of love. Even if it is a popular song, it's best for it to be performed instrumentally, so that there are no distractions to lure the congregation's attention away from the bride's entrance. This music should begin with a marked change from the previous selection so that the congregation can recognize its cue to stand as the bride approaches.

. . . .

JAZZ IT UP

Relying on the traditional simply didn't work for Veronica Chambers when she and Jason Clampet got married. Veronica says she had almost given up on finding the man of her dreams and was set on building her career when Jason appeared in her life. When he asked her to marry him, she was caught so off guard that her initial reaction was "No, no, no," so at the wedding she wanted to make it crystal clear that she meant what she was doing: She sequined the words "I do, I do, I do," along the bottom of her veil herself.

Rather than going for the classical Wedding March, Veronica chose "S'Wonderful," sung by Ella Fitzgerald, as a fitting testimony to her feelings for her man.

Using a Mantra

When George and I got married, we designed the entire ceremony ourselves. We knew precisely what we wanted, and sought to incorporate it in each aspect of our wedding.

SACRED WEDDING SONGS

Dunhill, "To the Queen of Heaven"

Hal Hopson, "The Gift of Love," an American folk tune derived from 1 Corinthians

Handel, "Let the Bright Seraphim" *Sampson*

Albert Hay Malotte, "The Lord's Prayer" (Matthew 6:9–13)

Mozart, *Exultate, jubilate,* recorded by Kathleen Battle

Leon Patillo, "Flesh of My Flesh"

Rachmaninoff, "Vocalise," recorded by Sylvia McNair

Gabriel Fauré, "Pie Jesu" (from *Requiem*)

Leon C. Roberts, "Let Us Rejoice to the House of the Lord," "Magnificat" (English translation, "Mary's Canticle")

Schubert, "Alleluia"

Bryan Thomas, "Heaven"

Maurice White, "Give Us This Day"

John Wimber, "The Spirit Song"

Wright and Forrest, "And This Is My Beloved"

As we were considering what music to play for our processional, we thought of our spiritual practice. We already had decided that we would walk together down the winding path of the Japanese tea garden where we were to be married, arm in arm, together from the start. We had African drums and Indian drums, a harmonium, a flutist, a keyboard player, and two singers. The music we chose to deliver us to our guests and altar was the mantra "Om Namah Shivaya," which means, "I honor the divinity that dwells within me." We thought that message was fitting for the moment when we would become one.

What we didn't expect was that the instrumental music would turn into a full-on chant. A number of our guests were also members of our spiritual community. As the music began, they naturally began to chant. Soon after, others picked up the words and were chanting as well. And so our entrance, our processional, was buoyed by the sacred words that had been supporting us for so long.

Vocal Selections

During the ceremony itself, when both bride and groom are standing together, sometimes a vocal solo will be performed. This song can be spiritual or secular, depending on your desires and the requirements of the ceremony site. When you engage a soloist, listen to the person sing your specific song in advance. Make sure that the person knows the words and the key in which you want it sung, and will dress in clothing appropriate to your event.

Occasionally, couples have soloists perform during the prelude period. This element of the music serves to draw the attention of the audience to the ceremony site, and gives them time to quiet down and assume an appropriate attitude for the ceremony.

SECULAR LOVE SONGS

These songs are among many that can be sung in most spiritual sanctuaries—with prior permission of the officiant. They invoke feelings of commitment and sacredness.

Luther Vandross, "Forever, for Always, for Love"
Kenny Lattimore, "For You"
Etta James, "At Last"
Heatwave, "Always and Forever"
Bill Henderson, "At Long Last Love"
Howard Hewitt, "I Do"
Amel Larrieux, "You Make Me Whole"

Recessional

The moment marking your union is a triumphant one. Let the music signal that abundant joy that overflows to your guests. Whereas your entrance was more slowly and somberly paced, your exit from the ceremony site should be upbeat and fast-moving. If you want to engage your African heritage, you can use drums to signal the moment of your marriage and have them usher you out. If you do this, you can hire a master drummer who works with you and your officiant to determine the proper moment to begin drumming. This can be after you have shared a kiss or softly as you are repeating your vows. As the officiant makes his or her final comments, the drums can grow in their power. Ultimately, they can usher in a jumping-the-broom ritual or an uproarious march out of the sanctuary you have created. You may consider hiring dancers to usher you in and out of the sanctuary. In this case, the dancers would appear from the sides of the sanctuary as the drums reach their crescendo. They would lead you out in a joyful dance as you recess swiftly, being sure to exchange glances with your congregation and each other.

❖ Readings

Biblical Readings

In Christian weddings, incorporating biblical passages is a beautiful way of invoking the sacred meaning of marriage.

1 CORINTHIANS 13:4–13

Love is patient and kind; love is not jealous or boastful; it is not arrogant or rude. Love does not insist on its own way; it is not irritable or resentful; it does not rejoice at wrong, but rejoices in the right. Love bears all things, believes all things, hopes all things, endures all things. Love never ends; as for prophecies, they will pass away; as for tongues, they will cease; as for knowledge, it will pass away. For our knowledge is imperfect and our prophecy is imperfect; but when the perfect comes, the imperfect will pass away. When I was a child, I spoke like a child, I thought like a child, I reasoned like a child; when I became a man, I gave up childish ways. For now we see in a mirror dimly, but then face-to-face. Now I know in part; then I shall understand fully, even as I have been fully understood. So faith, hope, love abide, these three; but the greatest of these is love.

1 CORINTHIANS 13:7

Love bears all things, believes all things, hopes all things, endures all things.

GENESIS 2:22–25

. . . and the rib which the Lord God had taken from the man he made into a woman and brought her to the man. Then the man said, "This at last is bone

· · · · · · · · · ·

of my bones and flesh of my flesh; she shall be called Woman, because she was taken out of Man." Therefore a man leaves his father and his mother and cleaves to his wife, and they become one flesh. And the man and his wife were both naked, and were not ashamed.

MATTHEW 19:5–6

. . . and said, "For this reason a man shall leave his father and mother and be joined to his wife, and the two shall become one flesh. So they are no longer two but one flesh. What therefore God has joined together, let not man put asunder."

1 PETER 4:8–11

Above all hold unfailing your love for one another, since love covers a multitude of sins. Practice hospitality ungrudgingly to one another. As each has received a gift, employ it for one another, as good stewards of God's grace. Whoever speaks, as one who utters oracles of God; whoever renders service, as one who renders it by the strength which God supplies; in order that in everything God may be glorified through Jesus Christ. To him belong glory and dominion forever and ever. Amen.

PROVERBS 18:22

Whoso finds a wife finds a good thing, and obtains favor of the Lord.

ECCLESIASTES 4:9–12

Two are better than one; because they have a good reward for their labor. For if they fall, the one will lift up his fellow: but woe to him that is alone when he falls; for he has not another to help him up. Again, if two lie together, then

. . . .

they have heat: but how can one be warm alone? And if one prevail against him, two shall withstand him; and a threefold cord is not quickly broken.

❖ Quotes

In addition to having loved ones read from the Bible, you also can invite them to recite quotes or poetry that speaks to your union. You may decide to write something on your own or draw from the resources of others.

We all suffer from the preoccupation that there exists . . . in the loved one, perfection.
—*Sidney Poitier*

Love takes off masks that we fear we cannot live without and know that we cannot live within.
—*James Baldwin*

Love is a special word, and I use it only when I mean it. You say the word too much and it becomes cheap.
—*Ray Charles*

Where there is love and inspiration, I don't think you can go wrong.
—*Ella Fitzgerald*

We must turn to each other and not on each other.
—*Jesse Jackson*

If you are wise and seek to make your house stable, love your wife fully and righteously. . . . Kindness and consideration will influence her better than force.
—Husia

Nothing that God ever made is the same thing to more than one person. That is natural. There is no single face in nature, because every eye that looks upon it, sees it from its own angle. So every man's spice box seasons his own food.
—Zora Neale Hurston

All you need in the world is love and laughter. That's all anybody needs. To have love in one hand and laughter in the other.
—August Wilson

Hold a true friend with both hands.
—Nigerian Kanuri proverb

❖ Poetry

Some couples find it impossible to express their feelings of love in their own words. This is where poetry comes to the rescue. Those bards of old and contemporary times offer their contemplations in poetic form, and this very poetry often captures the way that we feel about the one we are marrying.

For this reason, poetry commonly is included in wedding

ceremonies, just before the most sacred and formal part of the ceremony. It helps to set the stage for what is to come.

In order to find the poetry that sings to your heart, you will have to do research. There are hundreds of poets whose verses deserve consideration. Included here are the names of poets, teachers, and poems that are commonly used at weddings.

* Langston Hughes, our great poet laureate, wrote prolifically about the nuances of African-American culture and so much more. Among his great works are some poems that speak of love, including: "My Loves" and "Juke Box Love Song."

* Kahlil Gibran has many verses that people enjoy reading at weddings. Among them are "Third God," "Second God," and "First God," from *The Earth Gods* (1931).

* Nikki Giovanni, master poet of Black folks, has written a book entitled *Love Poems*. In it are several poems that are right for weddings: "Love Is," "And I Have You," "Resignation," and "A Poem of Friendship."

* Paula L. Woods and Felix H. Liddell (editors): *I Hear a Symphony: African-Americans Celebrate Love.*

* Joan R. Sherman (editor): *African-American Poetry: An Anthology,* 1773–1927.

* William Shakespeare, sonnet 116: "Let me not to the marriage of true minds admit impediments."

· · · · · · · · · ·

- Elizabeth Barrett Browning, "How Do I Love Thee?"
- Jalal Al-Din Rumi: *The Book of Love: Poems of Ecstasy and Longing.*

YOUR OWN WORDS

Have you written love letters to one another? Notes that you have enclosed with small gifts? Find those precious pieces of paper that house your sentiments toward your partner. Review your own words that you wrote in a moment of reaching out to your partner, and consider if any of those words deserves to be included in your ceremony.

❖ Rituals

Jumping the Broom

As far as my research reveals, the ritual of jumping the broom emerged during enslavement. Its exact origins are uncertain, but the most likely reason it arose is as follows. Our ancestors came from lands where ritual was primary in their lives. Marriages, births, death, and coming of age all were celebrated as rites of passage that the community must honor. When brought to this country through enslavement, they had no rights, including the legal right to marry. This was true even though enslavers often forced them to bear children who could toil the land.

Yet these strong people could not just make babies, and so they created a ritual in which the enslaver could participate. They took a broom, a benign symbol of householding. They decorated that broom and together jumped over it to indicate that they were married. Depending on the circumstances of their relationship with the enslaver, sometimes they would create a special event that truly celebrated their union. On some occasions, those who ran neighboring plantations had to agree that two people who "belonged" to each of them could come together as family, even if they continued to live separately.

Accompanied by a big-bellied West African drum whose beat invited the grace of the ancestors to attend the event and provide blessings, the two created a ritual that did indeed sanctify the moment. That they did not have a legal document binding their union did not matter. They had each other, in the company of their loved ones, their ancestors, and God to formalize their joining.

Today couples continue in this tradition, adding the ritual at different points in their ceremony, always recognizing that it

. . . .

is another part of our heritage of finding strength in even the most adverse conditions.

Something magical happens every time a couple jumps the broom. In those few seconds when they hold hands and jump together, with the accompaniment of the pounding of a West African drum, all time stands still. The ancestors have been invited to offer their blessings of strength and courage in the face of all adversity. God has been invited to bless the couple with all of the love and fortitude that they could ever need. Guests have gathered to witness this sacred moment of joining. And then the couple jumps.

For Fran and Bernie Jermont, the jumping-the-broom ritual occurred just as the wedding was ending. With Fran adorned in African garb and Bernie in a suit, this couple stood proudly before their family and friends. They had lived through two other marriages each and finally had found one another, believing they were perfect soul mates. When they jumped over their broom, they say that they did so for keeps.

In the years since their wedding, they have invited other family members to use their broom in their weddings. This tradition has special meaning because Fran and Bernie have taken in many young people who had been living in unstable family situations, and Fran and Bernie have become to them, as a married couple, an inspiration. Fran sees the broom symbolically sweeping out the debris of the past. The loving couple consider this sharing of the sacred wedding broom auspicious, because they remain happily married.

If you want to jump the broom at your wedding, here are a few key points to keep in mind:

- Select a broom in advance, and decorate it according to the style of your wedding. You can hire a designer to handle the task or design it yourself. George and I attended a couple's wedding in Tobago, in the West Indies, and George crafted a broom out of the dried palm leaves that were lying on the beach. Let your creativity be your guide.
- Many brooms come with silk flowers on them; incorporate fresh flowers on the broom if you can.
- Decide where you want to stage your broom-jumping event. Check with your officiant to see if you can have it in your house of worship. More and more houses of worship are allowing this practice, but you may have to talk those who are officiating through each step before they agree. If it occurs during the ceremony, a perfect time is just before the recessional so that the thrill of the moment remains high as you leave the wedding site. If it occurs at your reception, you may want to invite guests up to dance afterward to keep the energy flowing.
- Preserve your broom. Some couples commission Lucite boxes in which to frame their brooms. Others keep them in

a special place and bring them out once a year at their anniversary. Be sure to select a safe, dry place for your broom so that it will last throughout your life together.

* Write out what you want your officiant to say about the broom and its meaning to the two of you. Why are you choosing to incorporate this ritual into your ceremony? Answer this question in the form of a narrative that your officiant can read or use as inspiration.

* Make sure that your officiant settles on wording that will make the meaning of this ritual clear to all of your guests.

A Yoruba Tasting Ceremony

The West African Yoruba recognize that marriage does not promise a state of euphoria or peace on a daily basis, as every married couple knows. In their tradition, couples participate in a tasting of the four elements of life—bitter, sweet, sour, and hot—as well as water to cleanse the palate, as a way of demonstrating the fullness of experience that each married couple will meet with over time.

Typically, a tasting ceremony occurs before the bride and groom speak their vows to each other. A tray of the five items, usually cayenne pepper, lemon, honey, vinegar, and water, is placed on the altar or a side table. The officiant explains the reason for the ritual. The groom is then invited to feed the bride the first taste; she reciprocates by feeding him the first taste. As each item is tasted, the officiant describes the types of situations and circumstances that may arise that represent that flavor—for example, cayenne pepper evokes passion, whether the height of intimacy or of rage; the bitterness of vinegar represents the feeling of defeat that comes when a plan has gone wrong, a goal has not been reached, or a vow has been broken. After each taste, the couple cleanses their palate with water; the officiant explains that in this way, they will move on in the knowledge that together they can stand strong before whatever comes their way.

Communion

A Christian ritual that is frequently incorporated into the wedding ceremony, Holy Communion, is one of the seven sacraments. If your wedding is Catholic, the Holy Eucharist is considered the highest form of worship. The understanding inherent in participating in the Holy Eucharist is that you believe that the wine and wafers offered literally become the blood and body of Jesus Christ; only Catholics are invited to participate.

If your wedding is Episcopalian or another Protestant denomination, check with your officiant to determine to whom Holy Communion can be offered. Many couples choose to have Communion only between themselves, sealing their union in the most intimate sacred way. When this is the case, the officiant will follow the standard procedure of offering the body and blood of Christ to be accepted as a sign of the couple's acceptance of Jesus Christ as their Lord and Savior.

❖ Words of Wisdom

Although the length may vary, in every type of ceremony there comes a point when the officiant delivers some thoughts about marriage. Because you are choosing to have a sacred ceremony, your officiant will incorporate spiritual components as he or she describes the meaning and value of marriage as well as what the commitment calls for from two individuals.

If your ceremony follows a spiritual tradition, there will be a format that your officiant will generally follow. Particular words and phrases are common based on the tradition. Request a copy of the standard order of service including this section of the ceremony, so that you can make suggestions or ask questions about anything that gives you pause.

When you do not know your officiant, it is imperative that you spend time together discussing the ceremonial details, especially this section of the service, so that the content and tone of the remarks accurately reflect what the two of you value and how you look at the world.

Clarify with your officiant how you would like him or her

to serve this sacred moment, including specific topics you would like him or her to address. For example, if you have a child who will be entering the union, how will the officiant welcome the child? If you have a parent who has passed away, how will that person's spirit be invoked? Are there any special passages that you would like the officiant to read? The more specific you are in the planning stages, the happier you will be come your wedding day.

Ask your officiant to rehearse what he or she will be saying at your wedding rehearsal so you can address and discuss any changes that may need to be made.

❖ The Exchange of Vows

The pivotal moment in a wedding ceremony comes when the two of you declare your intentions to one another. For many couples, this is *the* sacred moment. It is the moment when you define what your marriage will be. Your vows may be a declaration, where you state your pledges to one another, or the officiant may ask you questions and you respond, or a dialogue, where the two of you talk to each other.

Start your contemplation of your vows shortly after you get engaged. Don't wait until a few weeks before your wedding. Now is the time to begin the inner process that will lead you to the essence of your commitment to one another. Check with your officiant to see if there are prescribed words that you must say based on the spiritual tradition that is hosting your wedding and if there is flexibility in amending those words and/or adding your own.

You will be facing one another as you speak your vows, and your congregation will be watching. Include them by ensuring that they can hear you. Practice saying your vows so that you are clear about where to place emphasis and how to project your voice lovingly. Find out if there is a freestanding microphone that you can use to feed your voices to the congregation. Some churches have microphones at the altar that hang from the ceiling. Other sanctuaries and alternative locations have no microphones at all. In this case, you may be able to secure a microphone from your ceremony or reception musicians for this purpose.

Speak your vows with confidence and clarity. Focus on your spouse as you say them. Speak from your heart. To be most effective, it's best if you memorize your vows. As "insurance," print your vows in large type (at least 16 point) on index cards. Give a copy to your officiant, who can prompt you with key words if you forget midway. You may also want to include a copy of your vows in your wedding program or as part of a wedding favor to be given to guests at your reception. One couple who got married in the Caribbean printed their vows on a scroll that was placed in a genie's bottle along with sand and rocks for all their guests. Let your creative spirit guide your steps.

. . . .

❖ Ring Ceremony

In many weddings there are two sets of vows. The second occurs when rings are offered, either in a single or double-ring ceremony. Once again you can repeat the standard vows used in a ring ceremony or create your own. The gift of a ring is a significant sign of allegiance and one that others recognize immediately as showing that your heart belongs to one person. What does the ring—or any other piece of jewelry—mean to you for your wedding? Will each of you wear a ring that symbolizes your union? How does your ring represent your marriage? Listen for answers from within yourself about the essence of what wearing a ring means to each of you, and add those words into the ring ceremony. Illustrate that love through your words.

Sample Service from the Riverside Church, Harlem, New York City

As you explore each aspect of your ceremony, you have an opportunity to blend in aspects of your cultural heritage, nuances of your unique relationship, relics from your family traditions, and words of wisdom that sing to you at this time of great joy. Let your love move you to design the most exquisite sacred event possible!

The Riverside service, which follows, shows how your wedding ceremony can fortify your joining in a sacred way.

• • • • • • • • • •

To the bride: _____ , *will you have* _____ *to be your husband, and will you love him faithfully as long as you both shall live?*

Bride: *I will, with the help of God/the Holy One.*

The following is for couples with children, in which we acknowledge the creation of a new family.

TO EACH CHILD BY NAME:
You are entering a new family. Will you give this new family your trust, love and affection?

Child/ren: *I/we will.*

To Bride and Groom: _____ *and* _____ , *will you be faithful and loving parents?*

Bride and Groom: *We will.*

BLESSING OF THE FAMILIES
Will your families please stand.

Do you come to offer your blessing and loving support to this marriage?

Families: *I/we do.*

. . . .

Blessing of Those Gathered for the Wedding

I ask all of you witnessing these promises to pledge your encouragement to the commitment that _____ and _____ are making today. If you will do this, respond by saying, "We will."

Response: *We will.*

Covenant Promises

Groom: _____ , *I give myself to you to be your husband, and I promise to love and sustain you, comfort and confide in you, and to stand by you in joy and in sorrow, in sickness and in health, in plenty and in want, all the days of my life.*

Bride: _____ , *I give myself to you to be your wife, and I promise to love and sustain you, comfort and confide in you, and to stand by you in joy and in sorrow, in sickness and in health, in plenty and in want, all the days of my life.*

Exchange of Rings or Other Symbols

Do you have symbols of your love?

Prayer: *Gracious God, remind _____ and _____ of your encircling love and unending faithfulness, that in all their life together they may know the joy and peace that grow from love and mutual respect. Amen.*

· · · · · · · · · ·

EXCHANGE:

Groom: _____ , *I give you this* _____ *as a sign of our love and faithfulness.*

Bride: _____ , *I give you this* _____ *as a sign of our love and faithfulness.*

WEDDING PRAYER (OPTION TO KNEEL)

Most merciful God, we thank you for your love that lives within us and calls us from loneliness to companionship in a world in which we learn what it means to be human by love responding to love.

As _____ *and* _____ *have chosen one another through the insight of your loving will, may they be protected from all harm and led forth in peace. May their love for each other be a seal upon their hearts and a mantle about their bodies.*

May your light surround them as they live into their promises. Grant that in a world that knows little peace and often seeks love in foolish ways, their life together may be a sign of hope that others may be assured unity and can overcome estrangement, and that oneness can help to resolve conflict, forgiveness can heal guilt, and acceptance can conquer despair.

Give them wisdom and discipline in their daily living. Encourage them to be true and loyal and caring. Nurture them in their work and in their companionship. Come to them and surround them in all the freedom of speaking truthfully.

May all present to these vows be renewed in their commitments and discover new strength and joy.

• • • • • • • • • •

We offer this prayer with confidence in your abiding love and everlasting presence as you have made yourself known to us in Jesus Christ. Amen.

PRONOUNCEMENT

_____ and _____ , you have committed yourselves to each other in this joyous and sacred covenant. Fulfill your promises. Live in peace. Love and serve God. Honor each other and all people. Know joy and blessing, for since you have united yourselves in faithful loving, I pronounce in the name of God/the Holy One, that you are husband and wife. Amen.

Ceremonial Rituals from
Around the World

*A*S WE BECOME an increasingly more global community, we discover wonderful aspects of different cultures that we can consider incorporating in our own lives. This is especially true for weddings, and particularly so when people choose partners who hail from other cultural backgrounds. Whether you are seeking ways to emphasize your African heritage, expanding your horizons with a partner whose heritage and upbringing differ from yours, or are simply curious about symbolic activities that you can consider for your wedding, you're in for a treat. Below are details from a variety of wedding traditions that may inspire your own sacred event.

❖ African Customs

Weddings throughout the continent of Africa are filled with ritual, ceremony, and drama. From the way that the bride and groom are dressed to the details of how they come together as one, many African couples even today draw on their ancestral traditions as they lay the foundation of their life together. Most common are multiple-day ceremonies that include a meeting of the two families, the offering of one or more animals for slaughter, fabric and money as dowry, sequestering of the bride and sometimes the groom to educate them on how to be a good spouse, the pouring of a libation, the playing of drums and other musical instruments, ritual song and dance, and a great feast.

Following Tradition in Modern Times

Niyi, a Nigerian brother who splits his time between New York City and Lagos, Nigeria, explained that when he and his wife married in 1997, the ceremony itself was held in the village where both of them were born, even though they and their parents now live in the city. They had two wedding ceremonies— a traditional one and an "English ceremony," which was a

. . . .

Christian ceremony. The traditional ceremony occurred over several days. Niyi had to visit his fiancée's family home to make a formal request to marry her. Besides himself and his kinfolk, he brought a cow, a goat, and a small amount of money, which together constituted the dowry. Typically, Niyi explained, the money is either accepted by the bride's father or given back with a blessing that the two will have a happy life together.

Niyi described his meeting at his fiancée's family home as light and friendly, (some families engage in a bit of sparring where the groom is chastised before an agreement is made for them to become one.) Part of this meeting included eating special foods—kola nuts and other symbolic foods.

Though both families lived in the city, all festivities happened in the village, and the cow and goat became the meat for the feast.

Ndebele Weddings

Some of the most elegant people I've seen are the Ndebele. Hailing from the south of Zimbabwe and parts of South Africa, these are regal people whose lives are an art form. Even today they follow traditional ways of marriage. The rites occur in three stages:

• The bride leaves her family home after a dowry or bride price is offered. During her time away, the bride must remain in seclusion for two weeks with female relatives, where she is instructed in how to be a wife and mother.

- When the first child is born, the wedding process is considered culminated.
- In the third stage, the husband formally honors his wife for bestowing him with so much love and abundance, giving her an assortment of gifts.

Tuareg Nomadic Weddings

The Tuareg people of the Sahara Desert believe that the blacksmith has powers of sorcery. It is he who announces the marriage. As is common throughout Africa, the bride is secluded for a period of time. She is adorned with ochre, and her body is smoothed with butterfat. An interesting twist on the wedding ritual is that when the bride leaves her maternal home, she cannot look back. She is leaving her family, and she must go with eyes focused forward.

Yoruba

A number of West African cultures, especially those in Nigeria, follow the Yoruba teachings. As African Americans have embraced African cultural traditions, many people here have begun to practice Yoruba philosophy. Here in America, there are rites of passage that individuals go through, learning how to be a woman and how to be a man, being taught how to honor the self and the family. In the Yoruba philosophy, the family unit is revered.

A traditional Yoruba wedding is a simple meeting of the families at the bride's family home; the culmination of a series of other meetings. The first is the formal introduction of the families. The groom's family introduce themselves to the bride's family and make the intentions of their son known. At this gathering, an appointed speaker for the groom's family, the *olopa iduro*, officiates, along with the *olopa ijoka*, the appointed speaker for the bride's family. The negotiations and decisions as to whether the union will be blessed occur at this time. Usually this is a formality, since it is understood that the two are interested in one another, but some sparring can occur to emphasize the seriousness of the moment.

This meeting is formal; the two families sit across the room from each other, and the officiants sit in the middle conducting the business at hand. A dowry is commonly involved. In the past, it was given to the bride's family, whereas more commonly now, it is given directly to the bride. To seal the meeting, the group eats ceremonial food, including kola and other nuts, honey, and sugar cane. Following this meeting there is a formal engagement gathering, also at the bride's house, and for this event family members dress formally in *asooke* cloth.

Before the wedding, the bride is sequestered among her female relatives and friends so that she can learn about the role of being a wife, and also so that she can become plump. Historically there were fattening rooms specifically for this purpose, because unlike here in America, where people worship thinness, in Yoruba culture and much of Africa a voluptuous woman is the ideal.

When the bride is officially married to the groom, she kneels before the groom's family to ask for their blessings and sits next to her husband. He removes her veil, and thereafter all are invited to eat a special meal. In traditional Nigeria, the two then go to the groom's home. The bride is scheduled to arrive before him and ceremonially wash her legs before entering the space. This washing of legs and feet is a ritual meant to represent cleansing her body before she comes to her husband.

❖ Caribbean Wedding Rituals

Many of us have direct and deep connections to the Caribbean. The Caribbean islands were a pivotal stopping point when ships of enslaved Africans were traversing the seas from the coast of West Africa to the Americas. The indigenous people who populated the lush islands of the Caribbean welcomed those who looked like them, as they were also overtaken by the Europeans who attempted to enslave them, too. Our histories run together with depth and meaning.

Guyana

In Guyana there is a fascinating custom that is immediately reflective of many African rituals, where the bride-to-be must be
lured out by the groom after he gets past her family. The
Guyanese stage what they call a *qwek qwek,* a lively gathering
that occurs the night before the wedding, when the groom
must visit the bride's house to stake his claim. Before he arrives,
the bride, her friends, and her family have a great time together,
sharing stories and preparing for a huge feast. When the groom
and his entourage arrive, however, the bride is hidden away.
Usually she is disguised in some way so that the groom cannot
recognize her. It is his duty to find her and claim her among a
sea of other women who pretend to be her.

While he is searching, a dance begins with a chant in Creole
calling out for the bride to show her face. When she is found,
the group gathers in a circle chanting and dancing with her
in the center of the circle. Often the chant gets fairly racy, with
the chanters making sexual comments about the bride. The
bride is then raised up on a chair and carried around the
chanters; this signifies that she has been identified and accepted
as the bride.

Much food and drink are shared among the revelers, and
the party goes on into the wee hours of the morning. Yet mirac-
ulously, everybody is on time and ready for the ceremony!

Bermuda

In traditional Bermudan weddings the bride and the groom are encouraged to walk after the ceremony until an archway called a moon gate is completed as a sign of good luck.

There are two wedding cakes, as in many American ceremonies. The difference is that the bride's cake is topped with a tiny sapling. After the wedding, the couple plants the sapling at their home, nurturing it as they are to nurture their budding union.

Jamaica

Like much of the Caribbean today, Jamaica is largely Catholic. Mixed into the Catholic ceremony are details that speak to the power of food in the sealing of a union.

No matter what other cake a couple have for their wedding, they must also have a black cake. This dark fruit cake, made with fruit that has soaked in rum for up to a year, often is made by a family elder. Eating black cake at a wedding is an auspicious sign of longevity. Many Jamaican couples today serve the black cake as the groom's cake.

❖ Native American Weddings

If you do a little digging into your family lineage, chances are you may find some Native American blood running in your veins. When our ancestors first came to North American soil, we often made families. Indeed, many West African men and women who had made their way to these shores shared the inherent quality in many Native Americans of loving and revering the earth and all that grows upon it. We bonded from the beginning.

Today, as we seek out greater meaning in our lives by researching our history, we often find Native American ancestors. There are interesting rituals to consider that are specific to different Native American tribes as well as some that are universal. Whether you are claiming Native American heritage or not, there are some wonderful practices that you may want to incorporate into your event.

Wrapping the Blanket

Sharon and Daryl Pendana staged an intimate wedding on the fourth anniversary of their meeting at a beach hidden along the Brooklyn shore. They invited guests to walk with them to the water's edge, where all gathered in a circle that Sharon and Daryl then entered barefoot. Sharon says, "We wanted to be in the open—God's cathedral—with the life-giving elements of air, water, and sun. We wanted to be barefoot, our feet connecting with the earth. We opted to walk together into the waiting circle of loved ones in a shared journey rather than me being 'delivered' to Daryl." They spoke their own vows to one another.

* * * * * * * * * *

In the midst of the simple joining ceremony that called on the spirits of the ancestors and God to bless them, their friend, artist and musician Jimmy James Greene, played an original composition on the violin, serenading their love, beckoning the heavens and all in attendance to bless them from that day forward.

Upon the pronouncement of marriage, Sharon greeted Daryl's parents and Daryl greeted Sharon's, then together they went around the circle greeting their guests as husband and wife. They honored a Native American tradition of elders having their mothers wrap a blanket around the newlyweds as a symbol of unity and the cloak of protection as the minister led a prayer for the blessing of their union. The group then walked over the dunes to the waiting wedding breakfast, where the couple individually seated each guest. After the meal, the honor attendants each spoke, and then they cut the cake. Each guest was then asked to select a small favor (stones wrapped in fabric and fastened with a small seashell) from a tray. Each stone bore a word the couple thought significant to marriage: God, love, tenderness, trust, caring, forgiveness. Sharon says, "We hoped that each person would receive a stone that would resonate with him or her more than a matchbook with our names on it. We felt certain that each person would, in divine order, receive the word that was perfect for him or her at that moment."

The Great Spirit

Native American culture on the whole has great respect for the spiritual life. Although they don't commonly use the term "God" to speak of their understanding of that all-pervasive power, they refer to "spirit" or the Great Spirit who presides over us all. In Native American wedding ceremonies, invocation of the Great Spirit is standard.

Water

Much as in Yoruba tradition, the cleansing qualities of water take on great significance at the time of a wedding. Brides and grooms often participate separately in a ritualistic bath, either in a fresh body of water in their neighborhood or at home using purifying herbs, to prepare them for each other. During the event itself, the two participate in a ceremonial bathing of their hands, a practice whose intention is to wash away any evil or lasting feelings from relationships of the past.

Music

Here's where nearly every tradition agrees: Music is key in the acknowledgment of a couple's joining. Drums, flutes, and other instruments are welcomed to emphasize the sacred and euphoric nature of the event as it occurs.

● ● ● ● ● ● ● ● ● ●

The Dowry

The sacred ceremony in Native American tradition occurs over an extended period of time, from the engagement to the couple's moving into either the bride or the groom's family homestead, depending on whether the tribal culture is matrilineal or patrilineal.

A key element in most Native American weddings is the gift of the dowry. Typically the groom and his family must bring food and money to the bride's family as an offering of his sincere intention to marry their daughter. The amount of money offered depends on the economic and social status of the intended groom. If it is not sufficient, the bride's family can turn him away until he is able to come with a sufficient dowry. The point here is to ensure that the husband is prepared and willing to provide a comfortable life for his new family.

The Pipe

At some ceremonies, everyone shares a smoke from the sacred pipe. Generally, the wedding officiant is the one who carries the pipe and shares wisdom from his tribe with all assembled. He offers blessings for the strength and loving kindness that this couple will experience in their union and passes the pipe for all to smoke to seal this invocation of the Creator's love and guidance.

Corn

Corn or maize figures prominently in many wedding rituals. Among the Navajo, for example, white and yellow cornmeal, representing the male and female, respectively, are combined to make corn mush, symbolizing the marriage bond. The Hopi incorporate cornmeal by having the prospective bride grind cornmeal and take it to the home of her intended's mother as an offering of her commitment. If the mother accepts, she grinds more cornmeal and comes to live at her prospective mother-in-law's home for three days. Throughout her stay, she continues to make cornmeal for the wedding party as part of taking on the role of wife in her new family. The corn, in whatever form it is prepared, serves as the bride's gift to her husband and his family as they start their new life.

❖ Islam

Many African people live based on the traditions of Islam, and many African Americans have either been born into or converted to Islam over the years. The wedding ritual that is part of that tradition is beautiful and loving. A wedding occurs over the course of several days and includes a number of rituals and involvements centered around family. It has several key components:

- *Mehndi:* This is the application of henna designs on the hands and feet of the bride and female members of her family that occurs a day or so before the actual wedding ceremony begins. This ceremony occurs at the bride's family home and is conducted by her female relatives.

- *Baraat:* When the groom arrives at the bride's home, it is with great fanfare as well as with a band of musicians.

- *Nikaah:* The wedding itself can be conducted at either family home, and is attended by close family and friends. The priest, known as the *maulvi,* presides over the wedding, and the father of the groom figures prominently in the event. This usually occurs on the fourth day of the wedding celebration. The *maulvi* reads from the Koran, and both bride and groom must willingly agree to marry. The dowry, or *mehar,* must be offered to the bride's family at this time.

- *Nikaahnama:* The bride and groom, along with the *maulvi,* sign this formal marriage contract. Family members bring the document to the bride and groom individually as they are seated in separate rooms.

- The jewelry given is either a necklace, a *lachha,* or a nose ring—not a ring for the finger.

- *Valimah:* The reception, sponsored by the groom's family. After the bride and groom are blessed, the festivities begin with dinner and prayers.

- *Rukshat:* The bride's leavetaking. After the wedding, the bride leaves her family home to travel with her husband.

· · · · · · · · · ·

◆ At the groom's home his mother holds a Koran over the bride's head as she enters, thus offering her blessings.

◆ *Chauthi:* The fourth day after the wedding. On that day the bride visits her family once more.

❖ Hindu

Perhaps not surprisingly, there are similarities between the Islamic and Hindu marriage rites, even though the religious philosophies differ. Among people who practice the traditional Hindu faith, the elements of the wedding rite are:

◆ *Baraat:* The groom arrives on a horse with a parade of well-wishers to approach his bride.

◆ *Milni:* The bride's family comes outside to welcome the groom and his entourage.

◆ *Var puja:* The bride's mother greets the groom by offering *arati* and flowers. *Arati* is the waving of a flame representing the connection between the couple and the divine.

◆ *Jai mala:* The bride and groom present each other with garlands of flowers strung together to represent their willingness to come together as one.

◆ *Sehra:* Someone from the groom's family recites a verse that introduces the groom's family to the bride's family.

◆ *Ganesh puja:* In Hindu tradition, Lord Ganesh is revered as

• • • • • • • • • •

the remover of obstacles; hence, an invocation of Lord Ganesh is offered to ask for a blessed union.

♦ *Bride's arrival:* The wedding occurs on a platform or stage, and the bride is brought there along with her mother's brothers and sisters.

♦ *Kanya dan:* The bride's father places her hand in the groom's hand, signifying his gift of the bride to the groom with all the responsibility inherent in that transfer.

♦ *Gath bandhan and phere:* To show the bond of marriage, the outer garments of the bride and groom are tied together at their corners. Then the two walk around the sacred fire together seven times as passages from the *Bhagavad Gita* are read.

♦ *Sapta padi:* As the couple walks around the flame, they repeat the seven sacred steps that represent the stages of their life together.

♦ *Sindoor daan:* To welcome the bride as his lifelong partner, the groom puts *sindoor,* a red powder, in the part of her hair.

♦ *Anguthi rasam:* The two exchange rings.

♦ *Aashirvard:* Those gathered shower them with flowers.

❖ Buddhist

One of the fastest growing spiritual traditions in the United States is Buddhism. From business executives to artists, people have become attracted to this Eastern philosophy. When it comes to getting married in the tradition, they look to the old ways, adjusting the elements to meet their current needs.

When following tradition, a Buddhist wedding would have the following elements:

*   The priest, or lama, recommends an auspicious day on which the groom's family can visit the bride's family to ask her parents if he can marry her.
*   To determine the date of the marriage, the couple consults an astrologer.
*   The engagement ceremony is called *chesiam*. During this ceremony, the maternal uncle and parents of the bride are seated on a raised platform, and the lama recites a prayer. He also distributes *madyan*, a religious drink, to all gathered.
*   A lama presides over the event that occurs at the bride's family home. Religious rites are performed, gifts are exchanged, and the groom's family offers the bride's mother a dowry equal to the price of milk.
*   Following the ceremony, the bride leaves with her husband.

❖ A Blending of Cultures

Being of African and Cherokee heritage, Bianca and Steve wanted to honor their ancestral roots in a unique way for their wedding without having to host more than one event. Though they lived in Brooklyn, they decided to have their wedding on

. . . .

a beach in the village of Oyotunji on St. Helena Island, South Carolina, a seat of rich African culture. Sixty guests were invited to the wedding, and all were asked to wear white. The couple also wore white—West African *boobab*s with silver embroidery—and white moccasins. Bianca carried a white rabbit-skin purse and replaced the usual bouquet with a turtleshell rattle.

They chose Yoruba priest and ordained minister Chief Alagba Igunfemi Adebalola to preside over their wedding. During the couple's engagement ceremonies in New York, the priest tested their compatibility, consulted the ancestors, sacrificed two chickens and two roosters, and released a dove, in the Yoruba tradition.

At the ceremony, Bianca walked onto the beach with a chanting entourage of female family and friends led by the queen of the village, Iya Orite. The entourage was organized according to whom Bianca knew the longest. The priest had asked the children to help put up the altar and to draw the images of an ankh and a circle in the sand. All of the guests and the wedding party stood inside the circle. The bride and her entourage circled the guests and groom three times before entering the circle. The entire time, Steve and the priest were chanting and dancing to welcome her.

The wedding included a tasting ceremony, and at one point the groom was blindfolded and told that whichever woman he found and identified as his wife he would have to

• • • • • • • • • •

marry. He found Bianca! He also was asked family-related questions, such as what is his mother-in-law's first name, to ensure that he was knowingly joining himself to the right person and family.

For the Cherokee elements, the couple looked to Hank Rising Sun as well as Bianca's aunt. Hank performed a ritual to the four directions, and Bianca's aunt performed a cleansing ceremony with a large fan made of blue macaw, wild red turkey, and pheasant hen feathers. During this part of the ceremony, Bianca remembers, seagulls began to circle over the wedding—a spontaneous response from nature that they believe was an acknowledgment of their union.

Before the ceremony ended, the two received spiritual names marking their union. Bianca was named Omitola, which in Yoruba means "water is enough, a thing of honor," and Ama, which means "water" in Western Cherokee. Steve was named Durojaiye, which in Yoruba means "wait and enjoy what the world offers," and Balogun, which in Yoruba means "leader in war."

During the reception, drumming and the Egungun dance were performed to invoke the spirit of the ancestors. Guests were able to visit the village and see the murals of the Yoruba Orishas (gods) that were showcased there. It was a great day.

Selecting Your Officiant

*T*HE MOST IMPORTANT participant in your wedding—besides the two of you—is your officiant. The person whose role it is to pronounce your union is the one who will either uplift the two of you and those assembled in describing the beauty of marriage or wreck the whole event. This is why it's essential for you to spend time selecting an officiant who can and will appropriately celebrate your joining. This person, the one who stands in the role of sealing the covenant that you make with each other, those gathered, and God if you choose to have a spiritual service, needs to know you, even if you only get to know each other for a short time prior to your wedding.

I emphasize this because many couples don't spend enough time thinking about what their officiant needs to know about them in order to craft an appropriate ceremony. Many details of both religious and secular ceremonies are pretty much set, but the sections of the ceremony where the officiant speaks about the couple themselves become powerful and moving when they are filled with the depth and dimension of the two specific and unique individuals who are coming together. So, dear ones, I encourage you to select your officiant carefully. Take time to communicate with him or her so that your desires are made clear. Request a written run-through of the order of service and script that the officiant intends to follow for your review.

The choice of a wedding officiant or celebrant depends largely on the type of ceremony you intend to have. If the event will be religious, the question is what religion or combination of religions you intend to include. If you both are of the same faith and denomination but don't attend the same church, for example, then you will have to choose one house of worship over another or an entirely different location for your cere- mony. Many couples choose to go where one partner has greater ties or is more active. It may be that the husband's church is better equipped to handle a number of people. If the couple is planning a destination wedding, an appropriate space will need to be found there.

When you take these various options into consideration, recognize that the officiant may change based on the location of the wedding. If you feel an allegiance to your officiant and you want to ensure that his or her message is heard at your wedding, you can make arrangements to use him or her. If the event is at a church, you will need to get permission from the house clergy either to include the outside clergyperson in the proceedings or have that person exclusively. Here's where timing and respect are essential. The way that you approach the house of worship where you intend to have your ceremony, especially about bringing in an outside officiant, will make all the difference in whether your dreams are realized.

❖ When Two Equal More Than One

I coordinated a wedding for a lovely couple who both have strong roots in their respective churches. In fact, the groom's father is a renowned preacher from Brooklyn, Reverend Herbert Daughtry of the House of the Lord Church. Danielle wanted to have her wedding in another historic church in Harlem, the Riverside Church, which is presided over by an equally renowned minister, Reverend James Forbes. Because the two ministers know and respect one another and the couple approached them in a formal and respectful way, their dream came true: They held their wedding at the majestic Riverside Church with *both* ministers presiding. They received counseling from each minister about the importance of marriage and its sacred nature in advance. They reviewed the order of service followed by the Riverside Church and modified it based on both ministers' requests as well as their own desires. What made the wedding extra special was having Herb's father present to make personal, loving comments to his son and daughter-in-law at the moment they became one. When he came around the altar table to embrace each of them, there wasn't a dry eye in the church!

❖ Interfaith Decisions

Many couples today come together as practitioners of different faiths. It's more common than ever before, even in the Black community, for people of different religious backgrounds to join their lives together. It's true that more African Americans practice Christianity than any other faith; however, many are from Muslim, Jewish, Yoruba, Buddhist, and other traditions. So, if you are Christian and Muslim, or Christian and Jewish, if one is Yoruba and the other Christian, what will you do?

You must decide together how you intend to worship as a

family. What faith will your children practice, at least when they are young? What practices will you include in your daily lives, outside of a formal spiritual environment? What aspects of your combined faiths can you bring to your wedding ritual to make it sacred and symbolic of your unique bond?

These questions are important for you to answer as you consider who will officiate your wedding ceremony. It's also vital for you to speak with your families about your religious differences in advance. In African tradition, the meeting of the families early on and continuously helps to ensure that any significant difficulties get ironed out *before* a couple marries. Follow this tradition now, even if you anticipate resistance. Be prepared to speak with your family about your love for one another and how you have worked through your religious differences. Articulate your ideas about how you will develop a shared spiritual practice at home. What your family wants to hear most is that you will be happy and protected in whatever decision you make. These should be your goals too.

❖ When Your Tradition Differs from Those of Your Families

As you mature and begin to make choices for yourself, it is possible that you may decide to recommit yourself spiritually to a tradition different from that of your family. What's wonderful is that you have found a pathway to God. What's challenging is that your parents and other family members may not understand.

In this case, it is your responsibility to set aside time to spend with your family members to talk about your spiritual life. Especially if you intend to incorporate unfamiliar aspects of your current spiritual practice into the ceremony, your family has a right to know and understand what to expect. If you approach them in a loving, respectful way with clear points about what you intend to do in the ceremony and—more important—how you intend to live your lives, they will be more willing to listen and consider your ideas openly.

I cannot express too much how important it is for you to enter this discussion from a positive and compassionate perspective. Put yourselves in your parents' position. They have reared you to have faith in a particular way. Now you have found a life partner and want to honor your union based on a philosophy that they may not know or understand. Naturally, they will be apprehensive, at least at first.

A Black woman who grew up in the United Methodist Church who married a Jewish man and decided to have an interfaith wedding came upon tremendous resistance from her family, even though her plan was to have her wedding at her family church. They were extremely apprehensive about her desire to marry a Jewish man who was also White. They felt that there were too many differences between them for them to build a strong bond. At first the woman was distraught. Together with her fiancé, they decided to refresh their approach. They brought both families together to meet each other and talk about their children. During the conversation, they introduced the topics of religion and upbringing. At first the discussion was a bit awkward, but the couple kept voicing thoughtful questions for everyone to discuss; tensions eased, and they ended up having a lively discussion. In the end, the families were able to agree that their children should be given their blessing to start a life together. They also found a rabbi who was willing to offer blessings in her family church, not a common occurrence in the Jewish tradition.

❖ When You Include Rituals That Are Unfamiliar to Your Guests

Part of the drama and significance of the wedding ceremony is the ritual. Whether the ritual is jumping the broom or sharing a kola nut, if you incorporate an unfamiliar activity in your wedding, your officiant's duty is to explain it clearly and artfully, so that everyone can follow and be an active participant in your wedding. This is true even if you have clearly described an activity or ritual in your wedding program.

Write out your understanding of the meaning of the activity, and present it to the officiant early in your discussions in an easy-to-read, typed format. Speak to the officiant to find out if your explanation suffices or if modifications are required. Request a copy of the final description in advance so that you are clear about what you are going to be doing and how it will be described. Though this may seem tedious, it's far better than being surprised on your wedding day!

❖ The Officiant at a Destination Wedding

Some couples choose to jet away to an exotic or remote locale to celebrate their joining. Whether for economic or creative reasons, when you choose to host your wedding at a destination away from your hometown, family, and friends, chances are the choice of your officiant will become a big question. Many resorts and spas offer complete wedding services, including a licensed marriage officer of the country or state. You can usually have your choice of religious or secular officiant even in remote locations. If you choose to work with a local officiant, I strongly recommend that you develop a rapport with that person as far in advance of your wedding as possible.

When two very busy New Yorkers decided to get away from it all and get married in Jamaica, they took their big plans and strategies with them. That included their desire to have a husband-and-wife spiritual team to serve as their celebrants. What they learned was that in Jamaica, they also had to work with the local minister for approvals and securing the license. The three ministers had to meet. There was a strong chance that the local minister might require that he actually conduct the formal part of the ceremony, allowing the co-ministers to share in only a small portion of the event. He was known to be concerned about preserving the sacred nature of the wedding ritual, and the only way he was going to turn over the reins was if the co-ministers could be trusted.

The good news for the couple was that they had chosen well. Michael Eric Dyson and Marcia Dyson are two prominent ministers and public figures in the States. When the three ministers met one another, they had a lively and relaxed exchange that put the local minister at ease. He gladly relinquished his right to handle the proceedings because he discovered that he could trust the Dysons to represent the teachings of the Bible accurately and effectively for this wedding.

The Dysons divided their duties, talking about what marriage means, how life evolves and grows over the course of a shared life. Since the couple both worked in the music industry, they used language appropriate to the nomenclature of hip-hop culture, driving home the point that even in the midst of all the glamour and hype of the entertainment lifestyle, marriage can live and grow if you choose to honor the vows you make.

❖ When Your Wedding Is Not in a House of Worship

People get married in backyards, on boats, in parks and zoos—just about anywhere these days. In some instances, the weddings are spiritual in nature, other times they are secular. Again, your desires and needs will determine who the right officiant will be. Religious celebrants frequently preside over weddings outside of religious venues. If you work with someone who is affiliated with a house of worship, you may be required to pay a fee for the officiant plus a donation to the house of worship even if you don't get married there. When you plan to use more than one officiant, an alternative location is often preferable, as some religious sites will not permit officiants of another faith to perform or participate.

❖ The Officiant at a Civil Ceremony

Many people think of a civil ceremony as a trip to the office where you get your marriage license or, rather romantically, as a visit to the justice of the peace. The reality is that a civil ceremony can occur just about anywhere, outside of a formal house of worship. It can include vows of great meaning that invoke your love and commitment for one another and requires an officiant who is legally permitted to marry people in the state or country in which the wedding is being held.

A civil officiant is equally as important as a religious one. In some cases, this person holds even greater responsibility, because it is his or her job to inspire the group gathered to recognize the sanctity of the moment no matter where the ceremony is held. Especially if the wedding is held outdoors, the spontaneity of the officiant is important. What happens if a plane flies overhead just as you are about to repeat your vows? A cre-

ative officiant will figure out how to pause gracefully and continue seamlessly, drawing on the events of the moment to bring
greater meaning to the event at hand.

If you select a conscientious officiant, even if you aren't
having a religious ceremony, this person can work with you
to make the event sacred. The officiant's tone, selection of
messages to share about marriage, and overall understanding
of the bride and groom as articulated to those in attendance
will all work together to create a sacred ambiance for your
wedding.

❖ Making a Civil Ceremony Sacred

When my husband and I went to City Hall to secure our marriage license—an activity for which both parties must show up
(no proxies allowed)—I noticed that alongside the queue of
couples was a tiny chapel available for those who actually
marry on that day.

Seeing that chapel made me smile. My understanding of
marriage is that it is a sacred act, one that calls for a covenant
with God. Even though marriage is also a legal transaction,
that's not what makes it work. The magic in a partnership
comes from the spark that's lit between a couple, one that they
continue to kindle and rekindle as time goes on. Invoking the

grace of God in that kindling is wise, no matter what the circumstances of the wedding.

If you intend to start your journey with a civil officiant, do so with a clear understanding that your union can still be sacred. Just as in a church wedding, you need to make arrangements in advance to ensure that the proper official is present and available to conduct your wedding ceremony. You will either have to bring two witnesses with you or request that witnesses be provided, often at a nominal charge. Speak with the wedding officiant in advance to learn about the content of the wedding ceremony offered there and to discuss your preferences. Often you can add or amend the content to reflect your religious affiliation as well as any particulars you have in mind. Give your wedding ceremony serious thought, even if you decide only days before to do it. This is the time when you are pledging your love to one another. Make the moment count by focusing on every aspect of it.

One couple shared that they met with the county clerk of their town, who would perform the civil ceremony. They reviewed the standard ceremony and planned several insertions, including a sung solo and a Bible reading by the groom's brother. They invited ten family members and close friends to join them at the appointed hour. Though they married in a government office, they designed a unique event, complete with a formal white wedding gown for her, a tuxedo for him, beautiful fall flowers, and music that they brought on CD. One friend brought a camera and recorded the entire event. When they later hosted a dinner for a larger group of family and friends, everyone was able to share in their joy because they had photographs of their beautiful day.

You also can get married officially at City Hall or whichever government office is appropriate in your town, and then host another function elsewhere with a minister.

❖ Alternative Locations

When you choose to have a civil ceremony rather than a spiritual one, it doesn't mean you are relegated to a government building. It means that an official spiritual officiant is not conducting the ceremony. To be clear, if you get married in America you must (in all but a few states) go through the civil process. You have to apply for a marriage license, and someone who is legally allowed to marry you in the eyes of the state has to make a simple statement of union and then sign the marriage license with you and two witnesses.

Surely, you don't want that to be all that your sacred ceremony can be! One way to personalize your event and give it your own sacred touch, even when you are using a secular officiant, is to host the event in a special setting. A park, an open field, a beautiful backyard, a yacht, a beach—all of these are romantic locations to stage a wedding. As you are considering locations, think about what activities, weather conditions, and decorations inspire the two of you. Work with your offi-ciant, friends, even a location scout in the city where you choose to marry, to help you identify a location that reflects your interests.

Writing Your Own Wedding Vows

CHANCES ARE you have considered, if only fleetingly, writing your own vows for your wedding. When I ask couples early on in their wedding plans if they are interested in writing their vows, most look up with a bit of surprise on their faces and then say, "Sure." It's a great idea that often gets pushed to the back burner. Securing the location, finding a caterer, working with a florist, and engaging a limousine service, not to mention organizing the wardrobe, all seem to take precedence.

Since there are vows that already exist in most spiritual traditions, and even for secular weddings, it's not an essential activity. And yet there is something beautiful and moving about transforming your feelings for one another into the words that you declare to each other in the company of your loved ones, your spiritual community, your ancestors, and God. Though the task may seem daunting at first, you have the opportunity to select words from your own reservoir of experiences, values, and beliefs about the life that you intend to build with your partner, words that can define your commitment. Whether you add to the tried-and-true vows that already exist or replace them, your own words can hold much greater personal meaning to you and your spouse as you cross the threshold into married life.

❖ Make Time for Contemplation

Finding the words to describe how you feel about your partner can be tough. Even as your mind and heart fill with feelings, a completely different mental muscle must be engaged in order to capture the words that best describe your bond. Here are a few contemplations that may guide you toward an inner vision of your union as you continue your inner exploration of your commitment. Each day you can reflect on why you are at this point in your life. What makes this time right for you to marry? By probing your own heart for specific answers, you will strengthen your union and discover how to describe it.

To prepare for your contemplation, have your journal and a writing instrument nearby. Sit in a quiet place where you will not be disturbed. Read the contemplation carefully. Then close your eyes and sit quietly, allowing it to settle within you. Breathe deeply and slowly at first, then breathe naturally. With each breath, invite your being to focus on the topic. Breathing in and out, stay with the topic. After a while you will relax. In this meditative state, stay alert. Notice if sparks of inspiration rise up. If you see an image that shows you exactly what you have been trying to explain, open your eyes and write it down. You may discover that several ideas come forth during your contemplation. Some may not seem relevant at all. Write them all down. Just as with dreams, you may not see the connection right away. Trust that the fruit of your contemplation is worth recording.

Later, compare your notes with your fiancé's. Do you see any themes emerging? Some couples have been able to compose poetry as a result of their contemplations. Others have found stories to share about one another that may not be appropriate for their actual vows but are great to include on a program or when making toasts. What's important is that you recognize the value in searching your soul for answers to how you feel and what matters to you about your relationship. When you treat your contemplations in this way, they will produce gems for you to incorporate into your festivities.

. . . .

CONTEMPLATIONS FOR EACH OF YOU

- When did I first know that you were my life partner?
- What was the first thing I loved about you?
- What is the quirkiest experience that we have shared?
- What are my beliefs about spirituality? What are yours? Where do they mesh?
- What characteristics do I love about you?
- How am I like my family? What behaviors and traits do I share with them? How do I feel about that?
- How are you like your family? What behaviors and traits do you share with them? How do I feel about that?
- How important is extended family to me?
- How comfortable am I with your family?
- Do I want your family to become my family?
- Who in your family is most special to me now?
- What rituals do I want to include in our wedding?
- What kind of wedding do I want to have? What does it look like?
- Who is part of the wedding party?
- What poem, quote, Scripture, song, or message do I want to incorporate?
- What is our song?
- Am I ready to get married?
- What makes me ready?
- Are you ready to get married?

- ◆ What makes you ready?
- ◆ Why do I love you?
- ◆ Why do you love me?
- ◆ How do I want to express my commitment to you—specifically?
- ◆ What is my intention for my life and our life together as I choose to marry you?

Give yourself time to do these contemplations. These questions require that you examine your heart carefully, honestly, and lovingly to allow the truth to emerge. Rather than feeling anxious or pressured about engaging in this activity, consider it a blessing for both of you. Don't force each other to plow through them. Instead, reserve part of your weekly wedding updates for a discussion of what your contemplations have produced. In this way, you both will have motivation to do the work.

❖ Creating Your Own Covenant

When Jocelyn Cooper and Christopher Halliburton decided to marry, they went to great lengths to ensure that they were conscious of what they were doing and to be clear what they wanted their union to mean in their lives. Both had been married previously. Christopher has two small children with whom he shares custody with his ex-wife. Jocelyn and Christopher's is

a marriage that involves many details, and they gave its beginning their all to pave the road to success.

During the wedding ceremony, they signed the following
document that they had crafted together, which outlined exactly what their commitment would be to one another.

Our Marriage Covenant

On this, our wedding day, we vow to continue to speak in love.

*We will continue to hold each other and treat each other in the highest
respect.*

*Speaking in love, we will continue to recognize and hold dear the taking
of responsibility for our individual lives.*

*Still, we will continue to take responsibility for each other; paying close
attention to and respecting each other's wishes, thoughts, and deeds.*

We will continue to honor our differences.

*And, we will continue to contribute to each other's growth, teaching and
learning from each other in love.*

Together we make this covenant; we will continue to speak in love.

Signed _____   _____
           Jocelyn   Christopher

You may want to craft something similar for your marriage. As
you contemplate what your union means to you, write down
vows that you would like the two of you to agree to fulfill. Be
mindful to keep the vows uplifting and specific. You probably

don't *really* want to force your fiancé to sign a document saying he will take out the trash every week, but you may want to include that the two of you attempt to resolve differences together rather than revealing them to others first. The goal of a marriage covenant is to create an umbrella under which you can find comfort, direction, and support.

For this reason, you may want to contemplate this question together: *What is my intention for my marriage?* Write about it in your journals and see what your contemplations reveal. The closer you can focus on your intention for the life you are building, the more stable your marriage will be from the start.

❖ Start Writing

Now that you have been contemplating the meaning and value of your relationship, it's time to take action. Begin to write down what comes to mind in phrases and sentences. First let the thoughts spill out on paper. When you find yourself stuck, look for words that paint a vivid picture of what you hold in your heart. Keep a dictionary and thesaurus handy to help as you search for the exact words to describe your feelings. Use these words to inspire your own if you like.

Verbs

The words that will figure most prominently in your vows are verbs. Verbs show action. They represent what you intend to

* * * * * * * * * *

do. As you think of your life with your partner, your goals and dreams, consider what verbs best describe what you believe your actions will be. Verbs that speak of commitment and love include:

- Pledge
- Vow
- Commit
- Honor
- Promise
- Devote
- Adore
- Respect

- Value
- Treasure
- Protect
- Celebrate
- Cherish
- Trust
- Love

Adjectives

Adjectives are used to paint a more precise picture of what you want to describe. They qualify our understanding of people, situations, and things. Think of adjectives that describe your partner and your relationship. Here are a few to get you started:

- Kind
- Thoughtful
- Enthusiastic
- Energetic
- Comforting

- Beautiful
- Generous
- Faithful
- Exciting
- Glorious

- Majestic
- Down-to-earth
- Friendly
- Awe-inspiring
- Trustworthy

Nouns

Nouns are essential parts of sentences because they stand as subjects, as that which takes the action. In a marriage, you and your partner are the nouns. You can use your proper names to describe yourselves as well as alternates. Consider these:

- Partner
- Friend
- Lover
- Soul mate
- Confidante
- Family
- Husband
- Wife
- Brother
- Sister
- Mother
- Father

Put Them All Together

As the words emerge showing you how you want to describe your partner and what you consider your union to be, you will need to put them into sentences and phrases that best express what you feel inside. Although you can follow any structure that feels natural to you, the general information you want to include is as follows:

• • • • • • • • • •

I ___ [state your name], take you [partner's name], to be my [wife/husband], and I ___ [state what your commitment will be, such as to love and to cherish], before God and [the ancestors, the elders, my family, and all the loved ones gathered, or however you choose to define the congregation] to be your loving and faithful [or other adjectives to describe your commitment] [wife/husband].

You can embellish these vows however you choose, adding sentences and phrases that accurately describe how you feel about your partner and what you choose to vow. Your vows do not need to be identical. You are two individuals, and your commitment to one another may be described uniquely, even as you agree that it captures in total the essence of your union.

❖ Traditional Wedding Vows

It may help you to consider the various wedding vows that currently are used in the most common spiritual traditions as a guide for your own words. In some instances you will see that specific vows are not spoken. In many cases the vows vary. I have included an example from various traditions for you to consider. If you decide to follow the vows of a particular tradition, speak with your officiant to determine if there are options and whether you can modify them if you so desire.

Roman Catholic

I, [speaker's name], take you, [partner's name], for my lawful [husband/ wife], to have and to hold, from this day forward, for better, for worse, for richer, for poorer, in sickness and health, until death do us part.

Episcopal

In the name of God, I, [speaker's name], take you, [partner's name], to be my [wife/husband], to have and to hold from this day forward, for better for worse, for richer for poorer, in sickness and in health, to love and to cherish, until we are parted by death. This is my solemn vow.

Protestant

I, [speaker's name], take thee, [partner's name], to be my wedded [husband/wife], to have and to hold, from this day forward, for better, for worse, for richer, for poorer, in sickness and in health, to love and to cherish, till death do us part, according to God's holy ordinance; and thereto I pledge thee my faith.

Methodist

In the Name of God, I, [speaker's name], take you, [partner's name], to be my [husband/wife], to have and to hold, from this day forward, for better, for worse, for richer, for poorer, in sickness and in health, to love and to cherish, until we are parted by death. This is my solemn vow.

Presbyterian

I, [speaker's name], take you to be my [husband/wife], and I do promise and covenant, before God and these witnesses, to be your loving and faithful [husband/wife], in plenty and in want, in joy and in sorrow, in sickness and in health, as long as we both shall live.

Interfaith

[Partner's name], I now take you to be my wedded [wife/husband], to live together after God's ordinance in the holy relationship of marriage. I promise to love and comfort you, honor and keep you, and forsaking all others, I will be yours alone as long as we both shall live.

Jewish

The sacred vow spoken in a Jewish ceremony happens during the ring ceremony. During this ceremony, the groom says, "Harey at mekuddeshet li b'taba'at zo k'dat Moshe v'Yisrael" (Behold, thou are consecrated unto me with this ring according to the law of Moses and of Israel). Following this declaration, the groom places the ring on the bride's index finger and the couple is considered married.

• • • • • • • • • •

Buddhist

Similar to traditional African weddings, the blessing of marriage comes with the consent of the two families under the supervision of the priest, or lama. There are no spoken vows.

Hindu

The ancient scriptures known as the Vedas are used to perform the wedding ritual. During this ceremony, the couple participate in the Seven Steps and recite vows that reflect each step:

1. May the Lord lead us to sustenance.
2. May the Lord lead us to strength.
3. May the Lord lead us to prosperity.
4. May the Lord lead us to the source of all bliss.
5. May the Lord lead us to good property.
6. May the Lord lead us to enjoy all the seasons and longevity.
7. May the Lord lead us to union, devotion, and companionship.

❖ Traditional Ring Vows

As there are sacred vows to be repeated within the ceremony that dedicate your love to one another from heart to heart, there are also ring vows that exist to demonstrate your commitment to one another tangibly. Once again there are very simple, traditional vows that you can recite or respond to as the officiant asks you standard questions. You can also design your own words that represent your feelings about the significance of your spouse's wearing a piece of jewelry that symbolizes your love.

In Roman Catholic weddings, the priest will bless the rings by repeating these words:

> *Our help is in the name of the Lord.*
> *Who made heaven and earth.*
> *O Lord, hear my prayer.*
> *And let my cry come unto Thee.*
> *The Lord be with you.*
> *And with your spirit.*

He will continue, "Now that you have sealed a truly Christian marriage, give these wedding rings to each other saying after me: "In the name of the Father, and of the Son, and of the Holy Spirit. Take and wear this ring as a pledge of my fidelity."

In Presbyterian ceremonies, the groom and bride each say, "This ring I give you, in token and pledge, of our constant faith and abiding love." And in Methodist ceremonies, each say, "[Name of partner], I give you this ring as a sign of my vow, and with all that I am, and all that I have, I honor you."

● ● ● ● ● ● ● ● ● ●

As you can see, the variations are slight, and you really do have room to describe your feelings for one another. Our African ancestors didn't necessarily exchange rings. They did give jewelry, sometimes beaded necklaces. Among some people, the gift was fabric. With each gift there was a ritual. You can create your own vows that speak to the essence of how you feel about your partner if you take the time to craft them now.

❖ Reflections of God

When Shiva and Rick Butler got married, they were entering into their union with their eyes wide open. Both had been married previously, and both knew that they wanted this marriage to last. Having seen the perils that occur in a marriage when you aren't ready or you aren't married to your true life partner, each of them wanted to make a fresh commitment to each other that would support them in the coming days and years as they became family.

In keeping with their spiritual tradition, they chose to use the words of the Siddha yoga meditation master Baba Muktananda as they crafted their vows. Instead of many other things they may have said or felt about each other, they chose to craft very simple vows that they repeated to each other: "I will choose to see God in you in our marriage." This profound message was enough for them, because they knew that if they chose to see the highest in one another every day, through the

. . . .

many ups and downs that inevitably will come their way, they will be able to stay together in love and peace.

❖ Designing Every Detail

Some couples choose to incorporate aspects of their mixed heritage into the wedding ritual. For Elizabeth Solomon, forty-six, and Michael Rice, fifty-five, this meant that they would include elements of her African-American, Native American, and Caucasian heritage along with his African-American heritage, including a Native American cleansing ritual called smudging. At their Cape Cod wedding, the smudging was led by Elizabeth's sister, a medicine woman. Using a smudge stick consisting of herbs such as sage, sweetgrass, and lavender, she lit the stick, and passed it along each side of each guest's body. The ritual represented the demarcation of mundane worldly life into the sacred. After this ritual, the keeper of the drum offered a special song that he had composed for the wedding.

The officiant then invited anyone who wanted to come up and offer his or her gift or words to do so. Each person came to offer a gift and to express the significance of giving the gift to the recipient. Elizabeth also offered gifts to some of the guests.

Next, the officiant led them into the offering of vows. They exchanged rings, after which the officiant pronounced them husband and wife.

After they kissed, they jumped a broom that had been

handmade for them. The handle was made of applewood, and the straw had been grown for them. The threads holding the straw together were burgundy and purple, the colors of the wedding. Elizabeth's sister and niece held the broom a couple of inches above the ground as Elizabeth and Michael jumped.

Elizabeth's Vows to Michael

You came into my life much later than I expected and I greet your love with a joy I could not have known earlier. You came when I was ready. And now you reside in my heart as if you had always been there.

Michael, I choose you as my husband, loving all that I know of you and trusting in the future of what I've yet to know.

I will build my life with you:
Nurturing your growth,
Comforting your sorrows and rejoicing in your happiness,
Sharing with you all my riches and honors,
Laughing with you and loving you as we grow old.

Will you accept these gifts?

Michael's Vows to Elizabeth

One day, one year to life
Remember

I am here, you are here . . .
Remember

We are here with others.
So they will know we are together.

I choose you to be my wife.

You are someone I greatly appreciate.
Because you are unique to me, you are special to me!
Leading me away from myself and to ourselves.

I care for you and what you do for me; I care for you and what I
can do for you!

Because you are my best friend, I promise to stand by you and
uplift you, so that through our being together, we can accomplish
more than we could alone.

I will work at being with you and always make you a priority in
my life. Your elegance and grace will be a delight to me always,
invigorating me to be with you.

Your insight, judgment will guide us through joy and hardship even when our way becomes difficult.

Our energies will invigorate both of us as we journey together.

REMEMBER!

The vows of various traditions and the specific commitments made by different couples have been included here to inspire you. Let your inner resources spring forth. Find the words within you to express your love and commitment for one another uniquely. Your effort will be worth it.

The Union of
Jocelyn Andrea Cooper
And
Christopher Dwyer Halliburton

Brooklyn, Prospect Park, New York

Celebrant
Rev. Eugene Callender

Processional
The Four Seasons - Vivaldi

Welcome

Family Remembrances

Rite of Marriage

Ring Ceremony

Acknowledgement of Children

Tasting Ceremony
Sour (lemon)
Bitter (vinegar)
Hot (cayenne)
Sweet (honey)

Presentation of Husband & Wife

Recessional
Piano Concerto No.3 - Rachmaninoff

"There is no remedy for love but to love more"
-Henry David Thoreau

Our celebration was enriched by your presence.
We are grateful for your love, guidance, and support.

Jocelyn & Chris
September 14, 2002

A. Cooper & Christopher D Halliburton

unite

You

Your Wedding Party:
Inspiring Others to Serve

HE DAYS AND WEEKS leading up to your wedding, as well as every moment on that blessed day, can be filled with experiences of joy and love. At this time, when you are joining with your beloved, you also are planning what many consider to be the most significant event in your life: the start of your life as one with another. This partnership will draw on the love and kindness of friends and family members. Indeed, those supportive people who fill your life are the very ones you should invite to your wedding. A few of them can be given special roles. As you consider how you want to design your wedding party and whom you will invite to be a part of it, take your time. Rushing into this decision would be a mistake. When you approach each decision that you make about your wedding with the intention of making your celebration sacred, you will be more precise in determining who would be best to fill certain roles.

❖ What Many Couples Do

When deciding who will be in their wedding party, many couples contact people who have been in their lives for a long time, whether they are cousins or friends, to ask them to stand with them during their ceremony. Because we often live in different cities from our loved ones, it's not uncommon that those people you've invited are hard-pressed to get to your wedding, let alone support you in advance of the date. That's not to say that long-distance maids-of-honor don't work. If a friend is committed to standing up for you and supporting you, she or he will find a way for you to work together. Otherwise, the members of the bridal party end up being just for show.

❖ Select Carefully

After you have decided that you will marry, spend a few days talking about the important people in your life: your parents, grandparents, siblings, cousins, and good friends. Think about what role each can play in your wedding celebration. Remember that everybody does not need to stand up with you at the altar during your wedding. Give yourself ample time, though, to figure out what needs to be done and the best person to handle the task.

❖ Your Family and Friends

We long to include the people we love the most in our weddings, but in some cases their presence may cause everyone major stress. The good news is that this is completely avoidable. When you hold your vision of your wedding at the top of your mind, your intention for the overall event as well as your focus on the details will see you through—even when it involves family and friends.

Most important is for you to be clear on what specific involvement you want people to have. Remember that your wedding is one of the most sacred rituals you will participate in for your entire life. Select wisely who will stand up with you on that special day.

❖ Who Is in Your Bridal Party

Usually couples select their bridal party based on how many friends they have and how grand or simple they intend their wedding ceremony to be. I encourage you to use different criteria. The people you select to stand up for you during your wedding should reflect the following characteristics:

- Love and respect for you
- A welcoming respect for your fiancé
- A willingness to accept and fulfill duties to support your big day

Parents

Obviously your parents will have a role in your wedding. This is true even if they are no longer a couple. If you have stepparents or another form of blended family, talk this through also, so that each parent can have a duty to fulfill as well as a place of honor on your big day.

- Parents usually help to pay for the cost of the wedding, though more and more couples today are getting married later and footing much or all of the bill themselves. Traditionally in America, the bride's parents help with the cost of the actual wedding, while the groom's parents host the rehearsal dinner and pay for the alcoholic beverages at the reception. If your parents choose to participate in any of these functions, make sure that you emphasize your plan to design a sacred ceremony. Let them know what that looks like to you before you start talking about money. In this way, they can help you to hold your vision, or you may discover that you need to help them come to a better understanding of what you want to do. In either case, it's essential to work through the details of what you intend to do and how they can help to make your dream manifest. Otherwise, you easily can end up dwelling in conflict over how the money that they are contributing will be spent.

- Your father can walk you down the aisle if you choose to follow that traditional format. If you are closer to your stepfather, you can invite him to walk you down the aisle. If you have a relationship with your father, though, it's important to let him know your plans. Each person deserves to be treated with loving respect, even when you choose not to invite him or her to fulfill particular roles.

- Mothers generally sit on opposite sides of the center aisle that defines your ceremony space. If you follow traditional protocol, an usher will escort the mother of the groom, signaling the start of the wedding. He will seat her on the right, facing the altar, followed by the mother of the bride on the left. Select uplifting music and a dignified usher who understands how to walk a mature woman to her seat. If your mother or future mother-in-law has a physical disability, make sure appropriate accommodations for a wheelchair, a walker, or other equipment are made.

• • • • • • • • • •

Siblings

Siblings take on a variety of roles in a wedding. Usually one or more will stand up with a bride and groom as part of the formal wedding party. Because sibling rivalry does exist and not every brother and sister get along, you may not want a particular sibling to serve in that capacity. That's okay. Again, what's most important is to talk to the person, even if you do so with a bit of trepidation. Out of respect for your sibling, you should tell him or her that you have selected whoever the people are for your wedding party. If possible, request that the remaining sibling be given another honorary role to fulfill—anything from shepherding children if the person is a parent or especially good with young people, to watching over grandparents, to greeting guests and handing out programs.

Friends

Friends come from all parts of our lives. There are the people who grew up with us; sometimes we maintain relationships with them over the years. Other times we simply remember them at important turning points. Some friends emerge out of our college years, fraternities, or sororities, new neighborhoods and jobs. Some people serve as close confidants, while others more accurately qualify as friendly associates.

As you consider who among these people will stand up for

. . . .

you, don't get stuck on sentiment. One bride's maid-of-honor was an old college friend. This woman, who was supposed to be the right arm of the bride, left the reception early because she had to go on a family vacation. Rather than receiving true emotional or physical support from the person who was given this honored role, the bride had to rely on her wedding coordinator and support staff to see her through the various challenges that arose that day.

Consider each person individually. Remember how reliable each was in past situations. Think about how the person interacts with others, especially under pressure. Who is a real go-getter and can buffer you when you need a break? Who has time and is willing to devote it to help you make your wedding a beautiful experience? As you answer these questions, your list will naturally come down to a few key people. Those are the ones you ask to be a part of your wedding party.

Coworkers

Coworkers often become friends, because they are the people with whom we spend more hours of the day than anyone else. That doesn't mean that every coworker should be involved in the actual ceremony or even be invited to the wedding. Think about the people at your job. Can you comfortably invite one person to fulfill a duty without offending the others? If you feel confident that there is a member of your work team who will

* * * * * * * * * *

stand by your side proudly at your wedding and support you as you need, by all means invite the person to participate. To avoid the spread of gossip, limit your conversations about the wedding to off-work hours, either at a private lunch or before or after work. A coworker can turn out to be an important ally during your wedding planning period, because this person truly knows your schedule, including how busy you are and when you do have free time to handle wedding details.

❖ The Roles of Your Wedding Party

It's up to you to assign specific responsibilities to each person you invite to be part of your wedding party. Surround yourself with people who are willing to take on specific tasks as well as be flexible enough to assume responsibility for something that pops up. The basic duties of the members of the wedding party are as follows:

Best Man

The best man's role is to ensure that the groom is comfortable, confident, and at ease. His duty begins the moment that the groom invites him to take the role, not just on the wedding day. He should call the groom regularly to check in to see how he's doing. Wedding planning can be very stressful for everybody, including the groom. Having a confidant with whom he can let off steam and talk about key issues is invaluable.

. . . .

The best man is often in charge of coordinating the bachelor party. As he does this, he must keep the groom's personality and intentions in mind. Some men appreciate the laughs and excitement that a stag party can bring, complete with dancing girls and alcohol. Other men prefer an event that's much more low-key and reflective. (Yes, some men actually have gatherings where they talk about what's happening in their lives and what their plans in the future will be.) The best man must also assess the groom before giving the go-ahead on any particular kind of event, and if he chooses to host an event where significant drinking is expected, he ought to schedule it a few days or more before the wedding so that the groom will be sober when he pledges his love to his bride.

On the day of the wedding, the best man stays focused on the groom and is attentive to his every need. This is not a time for jokes but for allowing silence to pervade when it's natural and a pep talk given when needed. The best man stands with the groom as he waits for the bride to come to him in the ceremony site. He also is the keeper of her wedding ring, and sometimes, in a double ring ceremony, both rings.

Maid or Matron of Honor

The maid or matron of honor is the right hand of the bride. Her role begins the moment she is invited to fulfill the duty. Her main function is to take care of the bride, to make sure that she feels comfortable, at ease, and prepared for her wedding day. No matter where she lives, she should call to check in regularly and visit the bride when she can. This can be done through telephone calls, e-mails and personal visits. Sometimes the bride has both a maid and a matron of honor. In that case, the two women divide the duties.

The maid or matron of honor usually hosts a bridal shower, often in concert with other friends or members of the bridal party. It is the maid or matron of honor's duty to find out what type of gifts the bride would most appreciate.

On the day of the wedding, the maid or matron of honor stays focused on the bride and her needs. If there are two people, she can divide up the duties, with one person communicating directly with the bride and the other facilitating any functions that may come up. The person who is most comfortable under pressure is the one who should be communicating directly with the bride.

The groom's ring is sometimes given to the person standing closest to the bride to be handed to her when the ring ceremony begins.

Other Members of Bridal Party

The other members of the bridal party also serve an important function. They have been invited by you to stand with you, because you believe that they honestly love and support you and

. . . .

your fiancé. Make it clear to them that these are the reasons that you have selected them, and ask them to stand with you throughout your planning. You will need to be specific with them as to what you need.

A person whose aesthetics you trust can be invited to help you figure out how to bring your wedding theme to life. Even if you have a wedding coordinator, it can be helpful to involve other creative people in the process early on. You can have someone help you gather fabric swatches, tear pages from magazines, and other visual elements that will make it easier for your vision to come together. Then, when you are ready to hire the professionals who will execute your vision, you will be crystal clear about what that vision is.

One well-organized person can be responsible for helping you to get all of the members of the party to go for fittings and get the various accessories they need for the wedding—on time.

Junior bridesmaids generally are members of your families who are preteens. They are too old to be flower girls but too young to be comfortable as regular members of the bridal party. These young people tend to be eager to help out on your wedding day in any way they can. They want to feel important, and will do their best to make your event a beautiful one. Consider inviting them to your various bridal showers. You also can ask them to oversee the signing of the guest book at your wedding and reception.

· · · · · · · · · ·

Ushers sometimes double as groomsmen. Whenever possible, especially for a wedding with one hundred or more guests, invite additional men to serve as ushers as well. These men help to keep the flow and energy moving before your wedding begins. For this reason, their personalities and dispositions are very important. Select people who are trustworthy, conscientious, well groomed, and cordial to serve as ushers. Tell them before the event begins exactly what you want them to do. Show them how you would like them to escort people into the wedding ceremony site. Decide if the space will be divided formally, based on the bride's family and friends on the left and groom's on the right, or randomly to fill up the space evenly. Assign one of the ushers to be the head usher and to work with the others to manage the gathering congregation.

If groomsmen also participate, have the head usher give them a cue for when they should stop their duties and proceed to line up with the rest of the wedding party to avoid a delay in starting the event.

❖ Others Who Ask to Help

Do you know the saying "There are too many cooks in the kitchen?" Don't let that be the story of your wedding. It's wonderful that so many people want to help out. In some instances, you may have a task for them to handle, such as helping to stuff envelopes when you are preparing to mail out your invitations.

• • • • • • • • • •

Be aware that even though people are well meaning, some can prove annoying, especially if you don't have time or energy to figure out something for them to do. Instead of agreeing to allow someone to help you, be clear and thank the person for the offer. Record the proper telephone number and e-mail address for him or her. Put the information in your official binder with your other planning information. Contact the person if you need help that you believe that particular person can offer.

I emphasize taking the time to figure out if a person is right for a task, because many hours have been wasted and hurt feelings have resulted from matching people up with the wrong duties. Something as simple as cutting ribbon for party favors can be disastrous if you give it to someone who has a short attention span or rarely pays attention to details. The little things count. To ensure that the spirit of your wedding remains uplifted and joyous, you have to act consciously, welcoming people into specific roles when it makes sense and standing firm when you say no if your heart tells you that's the right thing to do.

Keep in mind at all times that this is *your* wedding. The many people who shower you with their love and affection and who volunteer their time are doing so out of love for you. When you decide to say no to something that is offered, do so delicately and with compassion. In the same way, if a member of your bridal party does not fulfill an obligation, don't fret and stay stuck. Take charge. Speak to the person directly to find out if he or she will be able to complete the task. If not, find some-

. . . .

one who is willing and able to pitch in. You are not alone. You simply must manage the human resources at your disposal so that everyone is served.

Show Your Gratitude

The people who are standing with you for your wedding are busy, just like you. They have their own lives, complete with personal challenges, appointments, and people to negotiate. The point at which you decide to marry does not necessarily match up with the space in their lives when they have the time exclusively to devote their efforts to your cause.

So, even as it's imperative that you keep on top of your wedding party to be certain that various obligations are being fulfilled, you must remember to do so with love and an attitude of gratitude. Believe it or not, some brides have gained the reputation of becoming "bridezillas" in their pursuit of information and results from their wedding party. Trust that such behavior will only sour your relationships and likely do the very opposite of what you intended. People commonly stop responding when they are ridiculed or demeaned. Adopt the approach of appreciation. When you check in with people, first ask if you are calling at a time when they can talk. Keep your business brief. If you are calling a person who likes to talk about personal things first, do so, but make sure you let him or her know that you have a few agenda items that you want to discuss. Define the way that you will work together. If that means you will call once a week to check in, do so. Give specific assignments with clear instructions for fulfillment. But don't dish out orders like a drill sergeant. Be kind and gentle. Always say "Thank you." Show your appreciation through your attitude, your words, and your deeds. In addition to whatever gift you give your attendants at the time of your rehearsal dinner, you may want to get a little something along the way for someone who is working overtime to make your big day a success. Every thought, word, and action counts. Make all of yours count as reflections of your gratitude for the people who are supporting you so much.

Welcoming Children into the Ceremony

FREQUENTLY one or both partners come to the union with children from a previous relationship. That two people find love and want to grow it and include those children is beautiful. The challenge lies in determining how to include the children so that they feel welcome and at ease at this pivotal point in their lives.

Ask any stepparent of a child above three years old, and you are bound to hear that conflict looms close in their relationship with the child, especially if the child's other parent is actively involved in the child's life. Naturally, it's wonderful for both parents to take an active role in the development of their child, but the road can be tough for a stepparent to assess where the balance is and how to incorporate this child into the new family that is being formed.

Because the definition of family changes when children are involved, you need to spend some thoughtful time strategizing as to how to lay a solid foundation on which your relationship with the child or children can grow in your household as time goes on. If the child's father is not involved, for example, you may want to adopt the child so that everyone in the family bears the same name, clearly establishing that this is a cohesive unit. The foundation of family starts long before you join hands in partnership with your beloved, but at that point, at your wedding, it's wise to craft a way to welcome the child into the sacred bond so that he or she can see tangibly that you are building a life in which there is room for him or her.

What You Can Do

Think about the child or children involved. How do you spend time with them and include them in your daily life? Have the children witnessed interactions between you and your intended that demonstrate how you handle conflict? If the child or children are your partner's, have you been given permission to discipline them, within reason? What role will you have in parenting your spouse's offspring?

Many stepparents have expressed remorse that they didn't work through these details in advance of their wedding. Why? Parents often don't realize how controlling and possessive they can be of their children and how unyielding they often become when another—even if it is the spouse—steps in to address an uncomfortable situation with a child. Often stepparents experience the needs and desires of the children over those of the spouse. This can be enormously challenging for a disillusioned newlywed who once held the belief that, especially in a new marriage, the spouse comes first.

Premarital counseling can help work out some of the kinks in situations like this. You also can work together in this spiritual setting to determine how you want to structure your life to support your relationship with each other and with the child or children.

❖ The Ceremony

The age and maturity of the child or children involved will guide you in determining how you can involve them in the ceremony. Following are a number of solutions both traditional and more creative that you can consider:

- The classic ring bearer and flower girl roles remain great options for small children. Giving children the responsibility and privilege of being an integral part of the wedding

party will show them that they matter in your lives. Bringing the rings (although they should not be the actual ones!)
to the altar for blessing and leading the way for the bride by
sprinkling flowers along her path are important parts of the
ceremony that give your children positive attention. Take
the time to explain your feelings about the importance of
these roles so that the children can see how connected they
will be to you when they perform their duties. At the rehearsal, when they practice, pay attention to them and acknowledge their efforts.

♦ Junior bridesmaid or groomsman roles are great for preteens. In this role the children are invited to dress similarly
to the wedding party and walk with them to the front of the
church or ceremony site. If you believe that the children
will be fidgety, reserve seats for them in the front pews or
aisles. (This goes for the younger children, too.) Assign
someone responsible to watch over the children throughout the wedding and reception.

♦ Triple ring ceremonies (or more depending on how many
children are involved) are becoming more and more popular as ways to welcome children into a family. If you choose
to include your children in this way, make the ceremony a
two-part event. Your ring ceremony should be between the
two, as is traditional. Following that ritual, you can ask your
officiant to invite the children to come forward to participate in a family joining ceremony, where you commit your-

self to becoming family with these children as well as with your partner. In the event that your marriage does not last, understand that your commitment to the children must continue in some way; you must recognize your responsibility for their long-term well-being.

♦ Conduct a candle-lighting ceremony at the altar with the children, with the intention of invoking grace and acknowledging the presence and all-encompassing love of God into your family. Even the smallest child can participate with your guidance. In such a ritual, it's important that each child be given ample time to participate. You may want to invite them to develop a vow in advance that you work on together that they can state before lighting the candles.

♦ Plan to have a space away from the ceremony where children can go if they become noisy. Often there are anterooms in churches and other event halls. One of your ushers or hostesses can be in charge of hosting the children in this area.

Renewing Your Vows

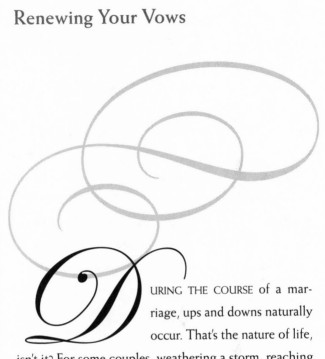

URING THE COURSE of a marriage, ups and downs naturally occur. That's the nature of life, isn't it? For some couples, weathering a storm, reaching an anniversary milestone, or just recognizing how blessed they are to have one another calls for a new celebration. Couples who reach the fifty-year mark commonly rejoice by enacting the wedding they never had or reenacting the one they remember, often for the benefit of their children and grandchildren, who joyously help to commemorate the grand achievement in high style. Another trend among Black couples is to renew

vows embracing cultural traditions. Many who married in a traditional Christian ceremony decide to wear African clothing,
serve African foods, and even jump the broom their second
time around together.

If you are beginning to feel that you want to renew your
vows, by all means do so. This is a wonderful way of honoring
the commitment you have made to one another and even refin-
ing that commitment to reflect where you are in your lives
today. It's best to plan this activity well in advance of your actual wedding date, because even though the two of you have
done it before, the work that goes into designing a wedding this
go-round takes the same amount of time! That last-minute gift
that you may have picked up to remember the anniversary
in years gone by isn't equivalent to a whole ceremony, unless
you decide to do it in Las Vegas. Even then, a little planning
can transform what otherwise might seem like a spur-of-the-
moment decision into a romantic moment neither of you will
ever forget.

❖ Refresh Your Resolution

When you decide to renew your vows, follow the same process
as couples do when they first decide to marry. Ask yourselves
the questions in "Reflecting on Your Commitment." Review the
trouble spots in your marriage. Search deeply, especially in

those areas of conflict or dissatisfaction that you tend to sweep under the rug. Talk through issues that have been troubling you, especially if you continue to harbor resentment about one behavior or another.

Seek vow renewal counseling. You can request the support of your spiritual adviser or a couples' therapist to talk through your life's joys and challenges. By doing so, you stand a chance of truly refreshing your resolution to stand as one before the world. If you find that there are sticking points that make you uncomfortable, don't worry. Every relationship has conflicts and challenges. You may be able to work through some of yours that have been festering if you allow them to see the light. Your counselor can help you to look at these issues objectively and lovingly, so that together you can discover how you will approach them in the future.

I mention this in all seriousness, because I know of some couples who decide to renew their vows for the show of it. They think it's a grand idea and go to great expense to have a big party. Yet something inherent in the renewal of vows always gives couples pause. It stops you in your tracks and demands that you look at what you are doing. For some couples, who haven't devoted the time to give a good hard look at their relationship, the renewal has been short-lived. Even after many years of marriage, some couples find that they have been harboring issues that suddenly rise to the surface. When the troubles go unresolved, they often blossom into situations that cause the undoing of what seemed like the "perfect" marriage. Give yourself the gift of counseling to fortify and strengthen what you've already got.

❖ Starting Anew

The magic of marriage doesn't always keep its brilliance as the years go by and challenges come to call. So it was for Natalie and Gerald Wilson. This couple decided to renew their vows in 2000, following three years of extreme hardship. During their trying times, Gerald went into a deep depression, which caused the couple to distance themselves from one another. After counseling, the Wilsons decided to recommit themselves to their marriage, particularly since, as Natalie describes it, they "made it through the storm." They chose June 17 for the ceremony because it would be their eleventh wedding anniversary. Reverend Emmanuel Holston of the St. Martin Church of God in Atlanta, Georgia, performed the ceremony.

Natalie knew that although she wanted a traditional Western ceremony, she wanted to wear traditional West African attire. She called on her best friend, Akitte White, who is from Liberia, to make her dress and had the remainder of the bridal party's attire designed and made by different West African designers in New York City.

The most memorable part of the ceremony was the procession. The attendants and the couple's four children entered to the sounds of a drum orchestra (their daughters played the maracas and their sons played small drums) performing Natalie's choreography. Natalie entered and joined Gerald to "The Storm Is Over Now" by TD Jakes. "As soon as I heard that song, I knew that I wanted it for the ceremony," said Natalie. "It tells a beautiful story and it applied to what we experienced. It tells you that in order to overcome trials and tribulations, you must not give in to all of the petty things you may encounter."

The actual renewal of vows ceremony was traditional, though the couple wrote their own vows, which focused on their uplifting, supporting, and encouraging one another, and which reminded them why they decided to renew their commitment to their marriage.

❖ Simple Yet Profound

Like the Wilsons, Kenny and Shunda Staples-Ray of Conyers, Georgia, had experienced a separation during their marriage. As anyone knows who actually separates, the chances of getting back together diminish when two people don't live under the same roof and when time ticks by. Not so for the Rays. They got married in 1990, split for twelve months in 1998, and after a year decided they were better off together.

In November 2002, they spoke with their minister, Reverend Julius Kidd of the White Chapel United Methodist Church in Conyers, Georgia, about having a ceremony during which they could renew their vows. The Rays realized that they had grown toward each other again and wanted to start over.

Once again they had a private ceremony. In 1990, it had been conducted by a judge. In 2002, it was held in their minister's private chambers with the couple's two daughters, Shunda's uncle, and a family friend as witnesses, because most of their family lives out of town. When it came time to exchange vows, they reaffirmed the ones that they originally spoke to each other, promising to be committed to one another throughout their lives. In the summer they hosted a large reception, where all the family could come together and rejoice in their happiness.

❖ A Surprise That Worked

When Oz and Lynne Scott got married, they did so with little fanfare. They stood with their parents, Lynne's grandparents, and her son. It was Lynne's second marriage and Oz's first. But that's not why they had such a simple ceremony. Oz explains, "I did not want to celebrate the *possibility* of our staying together. I did not want to put the expectations upon the relationship that wedding presents bring to it. The expectation of friends thinking that I'm giving you something to celebrate that you might make it."

Oz wanted to make it and *then* celebrate. And that's exactly what he engineered. When the couple had been married for twenty years, Oz secretly planned a grand wedding event to be staged within the context of a party that he and his wife were hosting at their Los Angeles home. When the two of them were dancing, Oz suddenly dropped to his knees and proposed. Lynne was shocked and delighted, as were some of the guests who were unaware of the plans. At that point, Lynne was whisked away by her friends to dress up and come back outside to participate in a traditional wedding ceremony. The couple's three children stood up for them during the ceremony. An AME minister who was related to a friend performed the ceremony, recognizing the sacred nature of their union and inviting everyone present to continue to shower them with their love and blessings. Each of the more than 150 guests held a lit candle to signify the group's support. In the end, Oz and Lynne got to have a grand wedding after all!

Things You Can Do

Once you make up your mind that you both want to renew your vows, you will need to make a few decisions, create a plan, and then execute it.

. . . .

- Pick a date. It may be your anniversary, but it doesn't have to be. Think of an experience that was meaningful in your lives together, one that strengthened your commitment, and consider that date for your renewal. Some people choose to invoke the ancestors to request a date, working through an oracle or other spiritual conduit. You also can pray together, asking for guidance on when to have your ceremony. Or you can simply select a date that is practical for everyone.

- Select an officiant. If you have a spiritual home, talk to someone there to find out if your pastor, priest, or other spiritual leader is willing and able to work with you. Talk with the officiant about your ideas on renewing your vows. Be prepared to discuss your life in detail.

- Plan the details. Do you want this ceremony to be Afrocentric? Many couples who had traditional Western-style ceremonies when they first got married choose to design their renewal events in a more culturally relevant way. You may choose other cultural elements to define your event as well, such as the rituals that you engage that speak directly to your relationship.

- Write your own vows. Especially now that you know what marriage is like and you have history with one another, it would be ideal to craft words specific to your union. Take time to capture the essence of your union in words, what

. . . .

you value and what you intend to sustain, and then offer those words at your celebration.

♦ Invite others to stand with you. You don't need witnesses for legal purposes. To invoke the sacred in the moment, invite your family members and loved ones who support your marriage to stand with you. Your ceremony can include as many or as few people as you choose. Just make sure that they truly believe in the value of your commitment to one another.

♦ Include your children. No matter how old your children are or if they are now part of more than one household, give each of them a place of honor in your ceremony. By consciously giving them roles of importance, including helping to plan the event, you will be honoring them as they honor you.

♦ Include the congregation. Among our West African forebears, it's common for everyone gathered at a wedding to serve as a witness to the great event. You can engage this practice in a contemporary way by asking all of your guests to sign a marriage document that you craft that invites everyone to pledge their love and commitment to helping you fulfill your vows.

♦ Make it legal. Some couples have lived as if married for many years. In this case, their renewal of vows includes a first-time legal declaration. If this is your story, rejoice!

* * * * * * * * * *

Even if no one else knows, it doesn't matter. It's not too late to go to the marriage license office together, apply for marriage, and then sign that document at your ceremony in the company of two witnesses and an officiant who has the legal right to marry you in that state. If you choose, you can declare your official marriage publicly during the ceremony to remind others that it's never too late to pledge allegiance formally to the one you love.

◆ Host a party afterward where everyone has a great time. The reception aspect of a sacred wedding is important, because food is considered to be the final ingredient that seals the couple to the community in love. To share your joy with entertainment, food, and loving communication is to complete the cycle of the sacred—going from the most intimate pursuit of your inner understanding of what you are doing to an outward expression of your joy. When you are renewing your vows, you have a perfect reason to welcome your community into your lives to celebrate your refreshed commitment!

You do not have to engage a spiritual adviser or host a special event to renew your vows. Keeping the promises that you have made to one another fresh in your awareness is a beautiful way of energizing your marriage. Some couples choose to repeat their vows to each other on their anniversaries. Others recall and discuss their vows when they come to mind. Whatever words you declare to your beloved when you marry are worthy of cherishing and remembering. Keep them close to your heart, and live by them together. Your life will be enriched by this conscious action.

• • • • • • • • • •

Starting Over

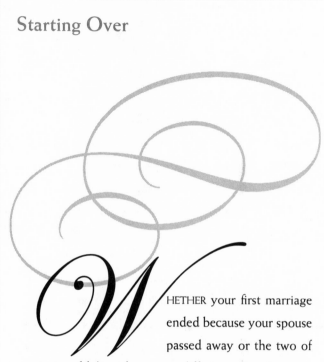

WHETHER your first marriage ended because your spouse passed away or the two of you just couldn't work out your differences, getting married a second or third time is not a surprise in our culture anymore. Even in the most conservative of communities, such as our own, the numbers have grown over the years. Indeed, quite a few people marry again and again until they get it right.

Tradition used to require that second (or third, or . . . weddings) should be more subdued occasions than whatever you had for the first. Society generally shunned a bride who had been married previously who would dare wear a white dress. The exception would be if the groom had been married previously but the bride had not; then the glitz and glamor would be welcome. Otherwise, a dinner suit for the man and woman were considered appropriate for a low-key, small gathering of family and closest friends.

Codes of conduct have relaxed significantly. Today, in most instances, you are free to do whatever you like. Barring religious restrictions, couples are creating all manner of events to satisfy their dreams of what their new life will be. Especially when a number of years have passed between marriages, people feel that this new marriage represents a brand-new lease on life and the potential for true happiness. So why not go all out?

You will have to decide what's right for you and your families. Just as with a first marriage, I highly recommend that you follow our ancestors' wisdom and seek out the blessing of your families. This is especially important when you are making the effort to marry again. I've spoken to many couples who have told me that they didn't heed the wisdom of their peers or family members the first time around. If they were young, the marriage may have occurred in defiance of their families. Marrying the community renegade doesn't usually work! If they didn't have a clear sense of who they were, people often found it impossible to find a rhythm in a marriage that could be sustained. And some people just grew out of sync in their relationships.

Consider what happened in your failed marriage before

• • • • • • • • • •

you enter another one. Look honestly at the experience to decipher the lessons that are waiting for you to learn. Do you truly believe that you know yourself now? Do you have a clear sense of your values and limitations as well as your expectations in a relationship? Assessing your life based on how you live and what you hope to achieve in a marriage is primary as you plan to start a life with someone else. You already know that you cannot change your partner. Are you willing to accept him or her as the person he or she is?

When you explore these questions, do so in your journal. Talk candidly with your partner about any reservations you have and any concerns you may be harboring about what didn't work in your previous marriage. Shakti and Rick Butler had been married previously to other people. As Shakti was contemplating her life and how she could approach her marriage to Rick in a more effective way, she consulted her father, who told her, "If you want the right person, you have to be the right person." She decided she would become the best person she could be, so that she could experience that powerful, loving relationship in her marriage.

As you plan your sacred ceremony, keep in mind the things about yourself and your relationship that you believe make you a strong couple. Make a list that identifies your strengths and areas needing improvement. Note where your views and those of your fiancé merge and where they differ. Discuss what matters to each of you in all facets of your life, including the ceremony itself. Work together to design your sacred event. In this way, you will be forging common ground well before you reach the altar.

❖ Our Way

When George and I got married in 1993, it was his first marriage and my second. The first time I got married in my hometown church with a huge bridal party and a reception in my parents' backyard.

I definitely wanted to do something different this time. I was starting anew and had the intention of designing a wedding ceremony that more intimately reflected the life that George and I had created. We had been together for three years when we married, so we knew one another well, and we shared a spiritual practice. I had learned a lot more about my African heritage and wanted to embrace that.

We designed a unique ceremony that reflected who we were and what we meant to each other. I wore a gown in the colors of the sunrise and sunset—brilliant oranges, reds, and yellows. We married outdoors under a tent in a Japanese tea garden. George collects crystals, and we brought all of them with us so that he could erect a sparkling monument welcoming abundance in our marriage, using every amethyst, quartz, lapis, and rhodelite he had.

When it came to walking down the aisle, George and I

· · · · · · · · · ·

walked together to the altar and our guests. We began as a team and continue as one. Each aspect of our wedding represented that teamwork, from the flame of life that stood in the center of the tent representing the light of God merging with the light of our love, to the seven sacred steps that we took around the flame—an Indian tradition that we welcomed thanks to our meditation practice—to the jumping-the-broom ceremony. We incorporated many aspects of who we are as a couple and melded them into our event. Working together was the thread that ran through all of the preparations.

Joining Ceremonies

*W*HEN TWO HEARTS come together as one and the two
are of the same sex, the
choices for how to honor your commitment can seem
limiting. In most states, you cannot legally marry, although domestic partners of any combination can now
usually secure legal documentation of their commitment
and allocation of resources. Depending on where you
live, that domestic partnership agreement can mean that
you have rights to insurance and other benefits depending on how the state, corporation, or organization of
which you are a part observes the partnership. Apart

from the legalities, what do you do if you want to honor your relationship in the fullest possible way?

In the Black community, ceremonies that celebrate same-sex unions largely have been private functions, well beneath the radar of the general African-American population. Why? As a rule, Black folks tend to be very conservative. Views about homosexuality and partnership have not been the most welcoming over the years. And yet, there are couples who find strength in their conviction and love for one another and forge ahead. It helps when they recognize and embrace a community of others who support them as they are. The truth is that Black lesbian and gay couples over many generations have done just that and have enjoyed loving, committed relationships as a result.

What You Can Do

If you are interested in crafting a sacred ceremony for you and your partner, do your research. Start by looking at your own life. Are you already a part of a spiritual community? If so, do you think that your spiritual adviser will agree to officiate a joining ceremony on your behalf? If you think this person will be open to the discussion, schedule an exploratory meeting.

During the meeting, be sure to address key topics, including:

- What type of service can you have?
- Where can your service be held? (Often, same-sex joining

. . . .

ceremonies occur at secular locations, such as parks, catering facilities, and private homes, because many houses of worship do not recognize the union.)

◆ Can you include any spiritual elements from your tradition? Find out specifically what you can incorporate.

◆ Can you write your own vows?

◆ Will the officiant guide you as you craft the program?

◆ Can the officiant recommend songs, readings, and other elements?

If you do not have a connection to an officiant, don't dismay. Look in the telephone directory in your city to find gay-friendly spiritual and secular advisers who are willing to preside over joining ceremonies. In the spiritual community, for example, some Episcopalian priests have called for liturgies for same-gender ceremonies. Check the local media that cater to the gay community for leads. Look on-line. And, of course, ask your peers for suggestions.

❖ Designing Your Ceremony

Like other wedding ceremonies, yours deserves your own special touch, with elements that reflect both of your personalities uniquely. Common elements include the exchange of vows; lighting of a unity candle that often extends to the greater community assembled; inviting those assembled to share in your union, and more. If you choose to honor your African heritage, you can include pouring a libation to acknowledge the ancestors. You also can jump the broom.

❖ Including Your Guests

One of the reasons that you invite guests to a commitment ceremony is to have them witness and support your union. At your event, be sure to guide your guests so that they understand their roles and help to make the event sacred. By all means, invite only those people who genuinely love and support the two of you.

- Invite someone to offer a preselected reading or poem.
- Welcome specific friends to make remarks about your union within your ceremony.
- Have the officiant invite everyone to stand in a prayer of unification before the ceremony ends.
- Present a special certificate that all guests can sign, indicating that they all offer their blessing to your union.

❖ Doing It Their Way

After two years of dating, Carla Grell and Shandra Williams of Union City, Georgia, decided that they wanted to seal their union. Carla, who is Trinidadian, was raised Catholic, and has a strong belief in vows. She had been in a previous relationship for ten years without a commitment and felt that a ceremony would be the best way to continue in this new and meaningful relationship.

The two spoke to their minister, Reverend Kathy E. Martin of God, Self and Neighbor Ministry in Atlanta, Georgia, who counseled the couple for six months before they decided to have the actual ceremony, during which she officiated.

The ceremony was held at The Magnolia Tea Room in Stone Mountain, Georgia. The couple, paying homage to Carla's East Indian culture, wore traditional East Indian attire, saris, and their hands and feet were dyed in the traditional *mehndi* wedding patterns with henna.

Members of the musical troupe Giwayen Mata drummed and sang as the couple entered, paying homage to their African roots. The ceremony included a ring exchange, lighting of a unity candle, and the lighting of four candles by friends for family, community, friendship, and spirituality.

Carla's parents, who live in Trinidad, were unable to attend, but her eldest brother, Gerard Grell, attended. Shandra's father and brother, J. Herbert Williams, Jr., and III, respectively, were also in attendance.

❖ When Baby Makes Three

The magic number was eight for this couple. When they reached eight years of being together and made the decision to adopt a child, Pepper and Michelle Heusner-Wilkinson thought they should formally recognize their union.

Michelle's father, the late Reverend Randolph Wilkinson, who was minister of Unity of Charlotte, North Carolina, conducted the ceremony, which was held in the backyard of their home in Stone Mountain, Georgia. That Reverend Wilkinson officiated came as a great surprise to the couple. He actually asked to do so, though they had not thought of asking him. Pepper's parents are from Belize, and though they knew about her life, when they arrived a few days before the ceremony, it was obvious that they were still a little tense. Michelle's father had a private conversation with them following the rehearsal dinner, after which they all seemed a lot more at ease.

Reverend Joel Blackford of Unity of Marietta opened the ceremony and Michelle's father led the remainder. Four friends, including Pepper's sister, Christine Robinson, and Michelle's sister, Linda Hayes, led a candle-lighting ceremony with the 110 guests before the couple entered the ceremony. Four candles were lit (for family, community, friendship, and spirituality). The couple entered the ceremony with both of their parents to "Let's Stay Together" played on violin. There was a gift of poetry and an exchange of vows and rings, the lighting of a unity candle, speaking of five reasons why God wants them to marry (including "to uplift one another"), a closing prayer, and the signing of the witness. For this aspect of the cer-

* * * * * * * * * *

emony, there was a board, which read, "United in joy on this day, June 23, 2001. Having gathered in joy and friendship, we the family and friends bear witness to their commitment. By our presence we offer our love and support." All guests were invited to sign.

END NOTE

I wish each and every one of you a blessed and joyful experience as you design your sacred wedding ceremony. I stand as living proof that it is possible to grow alongside a life partner, fortified by love and commitment. I am certain that for us, our wedding ceremony helped to anchor and focus our journey in life together.

Take the time to mold your ceremony so that it reflects your interests, similarities, sources of inspiration and joy. Welcoming the sacred into this moment can represent the essence of your commitment now and in the future.

THE CREATIVE TEAM

Harriette Cole, author and producer
Nadia Symister, executive assistant to author

Photography

George Chinsee, photographer
Lloyd Toone, photographer's assistant
Sharon Pendana, prop stylist
Kim Wilson for So Instincts, on-set styling
Marsha Ganthier, Nadia Symister, Regine LeConte, assistant styling

Floral Design

Kim Wilson and Aminah Yoba for So Instincts

Research

Nadia Symister
Regine LeConte
Marsha Ganthier
Amber Hopkins-Jenkins
DeLora Jones
Sienna Pinderhughes
Satya Simmons
Jarin Bakare

Location

Courtesy of Jocelyn Cooper-Halliburton and Christopher Halliburton

Credits for Illustrations (all photography by George Chinsee)

cover & p. iv: Cake topper by Ty Wilson at Zawadi Gift Shop, Brooklyn, NY

p. xiv: African horn, Eric Robertson African Arts; gold-leaf ankh, Zawadi Gift Shop

p. 4: Khamitic engagement and wedding rings, Studio of Ptah

p. 16: Khamitic engagement and wedding rings, Studio of Ptah

p. 34: Crystal decanter and goblet with etched Adinkra symbols, Zawadi Gift Shop; floral arrangements, So Instincts; candles and candelabra, The Harriette Cole Collection

p. 52: Afrocentric candles, BamboulaLtd.com; floral arrangements, So Instincts; ring bearer's pillow, Stuart's Creations

p. 86: Gold Sankofa comb, Zawadi Gift Shop, Brooklyn, NY; kalimba, Eric Robertson African Arts, New York, NY

p. 106: Silver tasting set, courtesy of Jocelyn Cooper-Halliburton and Christopher Halliburton

p. 122: Khamitic groom's wedding ring, Studio of Ptah

p. 142: Wedding invitation stationery, courtesy of Jocelyn Cooper-Halliburton and Christopher Halliburton

* * * * * * * * * *

p. 158: Floral arrangements and flower girls' baskets, So Instincts, Brooklyn, NY

p. 164: Organic stationery and CD, The Dress, The Shoes, The Invites . . . , Brooklyn, NY

p. 176: Khamitic engagement and wedding rings, Studio of Ptah

p. 182: West African drums, Eric Robertson African Arts and Sharon Pendana's private collection; broom, The Harriette Cole Collection

BIBLIOGRAPHY

Beckwith, Carol, and Angela Fisher. *Passages*. New York: Abrams, 2000.

Beckwith, Carol, and Angela Fisher. *African Ceremonies Volume 1*. New York: Abrams, 1999.

Bell, Janet Cheatham. *Famous Black Quotations*. New York: Warner Books, 1995.

Giovanni, Nikki. *Love Poems*. New York: Morrow, 1997.

Holy Bible, New Living Translation. Wheaton, Ill.: Tyndale House, 1997.

Mellon, James, editor. *Bullwhip Days: The Slaves Remember*. New York: Avon, 1988.

Peck, M. Scott. *A World Waiting to Be Born: Civility Rediscovered*. New York: Bantam Books, 1994.

Rampersad, Arnold, and David Roessel. *The Collected Poems of Langston Hughes*. New York: Vintage Classics, 1995.

INDEX

Abyssinian Baptist Church
(Harlem), 7
Adebalola, Chief Alagba Igunfemi,
106
African-American Poetry (Sherman),
71
African heritage, 17–35, 50, 105,
137, 140
honoring elders and, 30–33
how to claim, 19–22
invoking ancestors in, 22–25,
27–30
in joining ceremonies, 188
learning from, 33–35
music of, *see* Drumming
in remarriage ceremonies,
182
rituals from, 23–24, 66, 72–77,
89–94, 105–7
in vow renewal ceremonies,
168, 170, 174
African Methodist Episcopal
(AME) Church, 173
Akan people, 18
Altars, 57
microphones at, 80
Alternative locations, 118–19
for civil ceremonies, 122–23
for joining ceremonies, 187
Ambiance, 56–57
for civil ceremonies, 120

Ancestors
invoking, 22–25, 27–30, 74,
107
Native American, 97
Angelettie, Derek, 28
Anniversary, vow renewals on,
174, 176
Announcement, engagement,
13–15
Archer, Vimilakshi, 33
Arranged marriages, 33–34
Audiotape, recording family
history on, 21

Bachelor parties, 153
Bahamas, 57
Baldwin, James, 69
Barbados, 57
Baths, ritualistic, 99
Bermuda, 96
Best friends, spouses as, 44–45
Best man, 152–53
Bhagavad Gita, 104
Bible, 118
readings from, 67–69, 121
Black church, 17–18
see also specific churches
Blackford, Joel, 190
Black Power movement, 17
Blanket, wrapping, 97–98
Blended families, 148

Blessings, 84–85
   to four directions, 30
Book of Love, The (Rumi), 72
Boyle, Wickham, 52
Bridal party, 145–59
   children in, 163–64
   colors worn by, 58
   in processional, 61
   roles and duties of, 152–56
   selection of, 146–48
   showing gratitude to,
      158–59
   for vow renewal ceremonies,
      170, 175
Bridal showers, 41, 154
Bridesmaids, 155
   junior, 155, 164
   see also Bridal party
Broomstick, jumping over, *see*
   Jumping the broom
Browning, Elizabeth Barrett,
   72
Brundage-Johnson, Rashell-Lady,
   50–51
Buddhism, 104–5, 112, 137
Burkina Faso, 33
Butler, Shakti and Rick, 51–52,
   139, 181
Butts, Calvin O., 7

Cakes, wedding, 96
Callender, Eugene, 23
Calypso music, 26
Candles, altar, 57

Candle lighting rituals, 28–30
   with children, 165
   for joining ceremonies, 187,
      190
Caribbean islands, 80
   flowers of, 57
   wedding rituals in, 94–96
Carter, Janice and Dwight,
   44–45
Catholicism, *see* Roman
   Catholicism
Caucasian heritage, 140
Cave, Helene, 42
Ceremonies, 55–87
   ambiance of, 56–57
   children in, 161–65
   elders in, 25–26
   flowers for, 57–59
   joining, 185–91
   music for, 59–66
   readings for, 67–72
   ring, 81
   sample service, 81–87
   wedding party in, 145–59
   see also Officiants; Rituals; Vows
Chambers, Veronica, 48, 62
Chanting, 64, 95
Charles, Ray, 69
Cherokee rituals, 30, 105–7
Children
   adoption of, by same-sex
      couples, 189–90
   in ceremonies, 84, 106, 163–65
   of interfaith marriages, 113

from previous marriage, 129,
    161–63, 172
  at vow renewals, 171–73, 175
Choice, opportunities for, 39–40
Christian ceremonies, 91, 112,
    168
  Bible readings at, 67–69
  Holy Communion at, 77–78
  see also specific denominations
Churches, *see* Houses of worship
Civil ceremonies, 119–23
Clampet, Jason, 48, 62
Clarke, Caroline, 41–42
Clarke, Vera, 42
Classical music, 60
Cleansing rituals, 99, 107, 1
    40
Clothing, *see* Dress
Cole, Doris and Harry, 53
Colors, 141
  of flowers, 58
Commitment, 37–53, 79, 119
  changes over time of, 44–45
  covenant documenting, 130
  to giving, 51
  healing through, 47
  honoring, 47–48, 168
  and longevity of marriage, 49
  meaning of, 37–38
  of same-sex couples, 185, 186,
    189
  working at, 42, 46
  to yourself, 45
Communion, 77–78

Contemplations, 126–29
Cooper, Andrew, 29
Cooper, Jocelyn, 29, 129–30
Corinthians, reading from, 67
Corn rituals, 101
Corrective emotional experience,
    47
Cost of wedding, responsibility
    for, 148–49
Counseling
  premarital, 8–12, 163
  for same-sex couples, 189
  vow renewal, 169–70
Couple, functioning as, 44
Covenants, 85
  creating, 129–31
Coworkers
  announcing engagement to,
    14
  role in weddings of, 151–52

Dance, 90
  in recessional, 66
  in ritual, 30, 95, 107
Daughtry, Herbert, 111–12
Deceased parents, 79
  empty seats for, 29
Declarations of love, 42–53
Destination weddings, 111
  officiants at, 116–18
Disabled guests, 33
Divorce, 5, 38, 179
Domestic partnerships, legal
    documentation of, 185

Dowries
African, 91, 93
Native American, 100
Dress
African, 90, 93, 106, 170
for civil ceremonies, 121
for remarriage, 180, 182
Drumming, 90, 99, 107
invoking ancestors through,
24–25, 30
at joining ceremonies, 189
for jumping the broom, 73, 74
in processional, 64
in recessional, 66
at vow renewals, 171
Dyson, Michael Eric and Marcia,
117–18

Earth Gods, The (Gibran), 71
Ecclesiastes, reading from, 68–69
Egypt, 25
Elders
in ceremonies, 25–26
honoring, 30–33
learning about your heritage
from, 19–22
at prayer breakfasts, 41–42
reverence for, 50
Engagement
announcing, 13–15
Buddhist, 105
building bonds with family
members during, 34–35
traditional rituals for, 93

Entrance to wedding site, 56
Episcopal Church, 77
joining ceremonies in, 187
traditional vows in, 135
Eucharist, 77

Families
announcing engagement to, 13
blended, 148
blessings of, 84, 180
creation of, 49–50, 53
interfaith marriages and,
113–15
learning about your heritage
from, 19–22
Native American, 97
rituals involving, 90, 91, 93–94
Father, see Parents
Favors, 12, 98
vows in, 80
Fitzgerald, Ella, 62, 69
Flower girls, 61, 163–64
Flowers, 57–59
on altars, 57
aromatic varieties of, 58–59
broomstick decorated with, 75
for civil ceremonies, 122
in Hindu ceremonies, 103,
104
outdoor vases for, 56
visually beautiful, 59
Foods, ritual, 76–77, 91, 93, 94,
96, 101, 106
Forbes, James, 8–9, 111–12

Fragrant flowers, 58–59

Frazier, Veronica and William, 49–50

Friends
announcing engagement to, 13–14
role in weddings of, 150–51

Fun, importance in marriage of, 48–49

Gay couples, joining ceremonies for, 185–91

Genesis, reading from, 67–68

Ghana, 18

Gibran, Kahlil, 71

Gifts
at bridal showers, 154
ceremonial giving of, 140
to elders, 32

Giovanni, Nikki, 71

Giwayen Mata musical troupe, 189

God, Self and Neighbor Ministry (Atlanta), 189

Graves, Johnny, 41

Great Spirit, invocation of, 99

Greene, Jimmy James, 98

Grell, Carla, 188–89

Grell, Gerard, 189

Groomsmen, 156
junior, 164
see also Bridal party

Grounds of wedding site, 56

Guyana, 95

Halliburton, Christopher, 29, 129–30

Halliburton, Norman, 29

Hayes, Linda, 190

Heusner-Wilkinson, Pepper and Michelle, 189–91

Heyn, Dalma, 46–47

Hinduism, 103–4
traditional vows in, 137

Hip-hop culture, 118

Holston, Emmanuel, 170

Holy Communion, 77–78

Home-bound relatives, celebrating with, 31

Hopi, 101

House of the Lord Church (Brooklyn), 111

Houses of worship
burning incense in, 57
jumping-the-broom ritual in, 75
microphones at altars in, 80
music in, 59–60
officiants at, 110–12, 119

Hughes, Langston, 71

Hurston, Zora Neale, 70

Husia, 25, 70

I Hear a Symphony (Woods and Liddell), 71

Incense, 57

Instrumental music, 60–64

Intentions, declaring, 13–15

Interfaith ceremonies, 55–56,
112–13, 119
interracial, 113–14
traditional vows for, 136
Interracial marriages, 113–14
Islam, 31, 101–3, 112

Jackson, Jesse, 69
Jacques, Yvonne Jean, 42
Jamaica, 25, 117–18
flowers in, 57
rituals in, 96
Jazz, 60, 62
Jermont, Fran and Bernie,
74–75
Johnson, Ernest, 50–51
Johnson, Roy and Barbara, 51
Joining ceremonies, 185–91
designing, 187–88
guests at, 188
Journals, 7–8, 12, 181
contemplations and, 127
recording history in, 22
Judaism, 112, 114–15
traditional vows in, 136
Jumping the broom, 23–24,
72–76, 115
designing details of, 140–41
in joining ceremonies, 188
in recessional, 66
in vow renewal ceremonies,
168
Junior bridesmaids, 155, 164
Justices of the peace, 120

Kanuri proverb, 70
Khamitic teachings, 25, 26
Kidd, Julius, 172
Koran, 103

Lesbian couples, joining
ceremonies for, 185–91
Levin, Wilbur, 6, 40–41
Liddell, Felix H., 71
Love, declarations of, 42–53
Love Poems (Giovanni), 71
Love songs, secular, 65

Maid of honor, 153–54
Maize, rituals involving, 101
Mantras, 62, 64
Market, Richard, 46–47
Marley, Bob, 26, 27
Marriage licenses, 120, 122
Martin, Kathy E., 189
Matron of Honor, 153–54
Matthew, reading from, 68
Methodism, 114
ring ceremonies in, 138
traditional vows in, 135–36
Microphones, 80
Miller, Lisa, 28
Minor, Zachary, 52
Moon gate, 96
Mother, *see* Parents
Muktananda, Baba, 139
Multiple-day ceremonies, 90
Music, 59–66
African, 24–25

calypso, 26
for civil ceremonies, 122
hip-hop, 118
jazz, 62
mantras, 62
Native American, 99
original, 98
prelude, 60
processional, 60–64
recessional, 66
sacred songs, 63
secular love songs, 65
vocal selections, 64–65
Muslims, *see* Islam

Names, significance of, 20
Native Americans, 30, 140
rituals of, 96–101, 105–7
Navajo, 101
Ndebele people, 91–92
Newspapers, engagement
announcements in, 14–15
Nigeria, 70, 90–91, 92, 94
Niyi, 90–91

Officiants, 55, 109–23, 140
at alternative locations, 118–19
Buddhist, 105
for civil ceremonies, 119–23
Communion offered by, 78
at destination weddings,
116–18
for interfaith ceremonies,
55–56, 112–13, 115

Islamic, 1023
for joining ceremonies, 186–87,
190
music and, 65
and rituals, 75, 76, 115–16
traditional, 93, 100, 106, 107
two, 111–12
for vow renewals, 174
vows and, 80
words of, 78–79
Of Water and Spirit (Some), 33
Oliver, Reginald and Stephanie
Stokes, 48–49
Orite, Iya, 106

Parents
deceased, 29, 79
in processional, 60–61
role in wedding of, 148–50
Partnership, marriage as, 6
Peck, M. Scott, 39
Pendana, Daryl and Sharon,
47–48, 97–98
Perez, Lucille Norville, 42
Peter, reading from, 68
Photographs
of ancestors, 20, 30
of civil ceremonies, 122
Pinderhughes, John and Victoria,
45–46
Pipes, sacred, 100
Poetry, 69–70
Poitier, Sidney, 69
Posting the banns, 14

Prayer breakfasts, 41–42

Prayers
at joining ceremonies, 188
of remembrance, 30
wedding, 86–87

Prelude, 60

Premarital counseling, 8–12, 163

Presbyterianism
ring ceremonies in, 138
traditional vows in, 136

Processional, 60–64

Programs, 12
acknowledgement of ancestors
in, 30
large-type, 32
message to elders in, 32
rituals described in, 115
vows in, 80

Pronouncement, 87

Protestantism, 77
traditional vows in, 135
see also specific denominations

Proverbs, reading from, 68

Quotes, readings of, 69–70

Rashaida nomads, 31

Readings
biblical, 67–69
for joining ceremonies, 187,
188
message to elders, 32
poetry, 70–72
quotes, 69–70

Receptions
children at, 164
colors for, 58
invoking ancestors during, 107
Islamic, 102
jumping-the-broom ritual at, 75
vow renewal, 172, 176

Recessional, 66

Remarriage, 38, 48, 179–83
children and, 129, 161–63, 172
creating covenant for, 129–30
jumping the broom in, 74

Remembrance ritual, 30

Renewal of vows, 167–77
planning, 173–76
refreshing your resolution
through, 168–70
after separation, 171–72
to start anew, 170–71
surprising spouse with, 172–73

Restrooms, accessibility of, 32–33

Rice, Michael, 140–43

Ring bearers, 163–64

Ring ceremonies, 81, 85–86, 140
children from previous
marriages in, 164–65
Hindu, 104
Jewish, 136
role of best man in, 153
role of maid of honor in, 154
traditional vows for, 137–39

Rising Sun, Hank, 107

Rituals, 72–78, 89–107
African, 23–24, 72–77

blending cultures, 105–7
Buddhist, 104–5
candle-lighting, 28–30, 165
Caribbean, 94–96
Christian, 77–78
Hindu, 103–4
Islamic, 101–3
Native American, 96–101, 140
remembrance, 30
unfamiliar, 115–16
for vow renewals, 174
see also Jumping the broom
Riverside Church (Harlem), 8, 111
sample service from, 81–87
Road Less Traveled, A (Peck), 39
Robinson, Christine, 190
Robinson, Frank and Nancy, 50
Roman Catholicism, 14, 77, 96
ring ceremonies in, 138
traditional vows in, 135, 188
Rumi, Jalal Al-Din, 72

Sacred wedding songs, 63
Sahara Desert, Tuareg nomads of, 92
St. Martin Church of God (Atlanta), 170
Same-sex couples, joining ceremonies for, 185–91
Sankofa symbol, 18, 19
Scott, Oz and Lynn, 47, 172–73
Seats
for elders, 32
held for deceased parents, 29

Second marriages, *see* Remarriage
Secular love songs, 65
Separation, renewal of vows after, 171–72
Shakespeare, William, 71
Sherman, Joan R., 71
Siblings, role in weddings of, 150
Siddha yoga, 139
Smudging, 140
Soloists, songs sung by, 64–65, 121
Solomon, Elizabeth, 140–43
Some, Malidoma, 33
Songs, 121
for joining ceremonies, 187
ritual, 90
sacred, 63
secular, 65
South Africa, 91
Spiritual journey, 38–39
Staples-Ray, Kenny and Shunda, 171–72
Stepparents, 148, 149, 161–63
Sudan, 25
Symister, Hatshepsut and Richard, 25

Tasting ceremonies, Yoruba, 76–77, 106
Tents, 56
Tobago, 75
Toone, Peggy Dillard and Lloyd, 43–44

Trinidad, 188, 189

Tuareg people, 92

Understanding, mutual, 53

Unity candle, 28–29

Ushers, 156

  see also Bridal party

Vases, outdoor, 56

Vedas, 137

Videotape, recording family

  history on, 21

Vocal music, 64–65

Vows, 12, 125–43

  at civil ceremonies, 119

  contemplation of, 126–29

  creation of covenant for,

    129–31

  designing details of, 140–41

  exchange of, 79–80

  for joining ceremonies, 187

  meaning of, 45

  pre-eminence of, 43–44

  reflections of God in, 139–40

  renewing, *see* Renewal of vows

  for ring ceremonies, 81, 137–39

  traditional, 134–37

  writing, 131–34, 174–75

Ward, Charles and Cheryl, 53

Water, ritual cleansing qualities of,

  99

Wedding party, *see* Bridal party

White, Akitte, 170

White Chapel United Methodist

  Church (Conyers, Georgia),

  172

Widowhood, 53, 179

Wiles, Olga, 42

Wilkinson, Randolph, 190

Williams, J. Herbert, 189

Williams, Shandra, 188–89

Wilson, August, 70

Wilson, Natalie and Gerald,

  170–71

Witnesses, 121, 122, 175

  to joining ceremonies, 190–91

Woods, Paula L., 71

Wrapping the blanket, 97–98

Wright, Gloria, 42

Yoga, 139

Yoruba tradition, 26, 92–94, 99,

  106–7, 112

  tasting ceremonies, 76–77,

  106

Zangrillo, Alexandra Sanidad and

  Vincent, 51

Zimbabwe, 91